DR. KAR

Your Untapped Source

Discovering Your
Kingdom Position

Suwanee, Georgia

First published by Faith Books & MORE
ISBN 978-0-9860159-9-1

Printed in the United States of America.

This book is printed on acid-free paper.

3255 Lawrenceville-Suwanee Rd.
Suite P250
Suwanee, GA 30024
publishing@faithbooksandmore.com
www.faithbooksandmore.com

TABLE OF CONTENTS

FOREWORD

Dr. Samuel R. Chand
Author, *Cracking Your Church's Culture Code*
www.samchand.com

In this dynamic book you will have the opportunity to discover the secret to spiritual fulfillment as well as understand your unending flow of personal significance by knowing how you have been positioned by God in His Kingdom. Realization of dreams and the unleashing of eternal power are placed within you once you grasp the Kingdom dynamic of the life of Christ.

This book has been written with a spirit-filled compassion to see that every believer walks in their divine purpose totally and without apology. Dr. Smith believes in developing, training, and building people, and has devoted her life to this cause. This book was written to direct men and women to a path of Kingdom living and freedom from the chains of ineptitude and mediocrity, becoming the accomplished persons God intends them to be. This work endeavors to be a bridge reconnecting you with your true self, just as God created and sees you.

God does not want His Kingdom shrouded in ambiguity and mystery. He wants His saints to gain fluency concerning His culture and His ways of doing things so His Kingdom can rule on earth as it already reigns in heaven.

This charge is not for the complacent individual or

corporate body, but for those who are willing to push past traditions and status quo, the weird and the impotent, in order to seize the world where God reigns. It certainly is His good pleasure to give us the Kingdom!

There is truly more to this life; there is a more adventurous set of circumstances for you, and you don't have to settle for the routine of merely existing. You will find in this book the opportunity to live vigorously and to flourish. This is the impregnable time to allow the knowledge and understanding of God's Kingdom to dictate every sphere of your life, your future, and your bloodline.

Your Untapped Source: Discovering Your Kingdom Position is a work that challenges us to respond to the call of the Kingdom— to know it, understand it, walk in it, and advance it so there can be global impact of epic proportions for God's program here on earth.

Dr. Samuel R. Chand
Author, *Cracking Your Church's Culture Code*
www.samchand.com

ACKNOWLEDGMENTS

I wish to acknowledge those of my life who directly and indirectly inspired this book with all the nuances of Kingdom living. My parents, with their tireless dedication to God and ministry bringing up children in a world that says there is no God, constantly exposed me to church and to a world outside this physical place where we live.

I also wish to acknowledge the spiritual laborers in my life such as my pastor and many Kingdom believers around me who work before the Lord Christ to bring a fresh word of life-changing proportions to the world. Without their unceasing dedication to the proponents of the Kingdom concept, I would not be where I am today. The apostolic and prophetic mantle on these believers' lives reaches to the local and international community, directly to the heart and soul of the body of Christ. In this, we are positioned to reach the world for the advancement of God's Kingdom.

This book is the product of many people who have continued to change my life and push me into divine destiny. I pray that God's Kingdom may come in and through you and your bloodline.

INTRODUCTION

It is critical to explore the multi-dimensional and comprehensive aspect of the Kingdom of God. It is said the Kingdom of God takes on many diversifications in the practice of the Church. Consequently, due to a limited understanding of the Kingdom, the church fails to walk in all its true dimensions. Jesus Christ, the Son of God sent by His Father-God to redeem and to restore mankind back into right relationship with God, proclaimed clearly that "the Kingdom of God is within you" (Luke 17:21 NKJV). With further explanation, Jesus vehemently expounded that the Kingdom of God was not only within man, but also that it was at hand (Mark 1:14, 15).

Jesus also endeavored to instruct the synagogue leaders and scribes that for which they had for centuries searched and studied of the prophets of old was now manifested or come to pass (John 1:45; 49). Christ—the Anointed One from God—proclaimed that He only spoke what he heard the Father speak and only did what the Father did (John 5:19). The Father was announcing that the Kingdom age had fully appeared, spearheaded by Jesus Himself; an age of living, being, and doing manifested on the earth.

It is from these proclamations that Kingdom of God consciousness now comes to empower the heart of every believer with a transformed awareness in order to carry out God's divine will on the earth. This examination will unveil and establish that perception of the Kingdom of God is needed to fulfill the mandated will of God and to live a victorious life in Christ Jesus (a life submitted to the laws and

commandments of God). Therefore, it is necessary to understand the Kingdom of God in light of the developmental process of the believer's realization. This process will begin from a world ideology, proceeding to a church philosophy, and finally arriving at Kingdom of God consciousness. This Kingdom cognizance results in a revolutionary mindset in which the Holy Spirit aids the believer to discover his divine identity and the power given him through the sacrificial act of Jesus Christ on the cross. This Kingdom apprehension is the catalyst for living out a victorious life and the divine will of God for all who believe.

Dr. Karen M. Smith

Section 1

Chapter 1

DEFINING THE KINGDOM OF GOD

The Kingdom of God is the realm where and how God rules. The different components of the Kingdom of God categorize God's methodological way of communicating His plan and sovereign will to every believer. This way of living and thinking in the earth transcends the established order of world government, economics, politics, and even religion.

This spiritual, governmental dimension is the model by which mankind may understand the concept of ruling and reigning on earth through Christ, which is God's ultimate purpose for those who believe in Him. It is not only about advancing in economics and political power; nor is it about securing geographical territory. God's aim is the heart of mankind. Author and national teacher

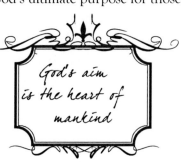

God's aim is the heart of mankind

Myles Munroe, in his book, *Rediscovering the Kingdom*, iterates: "It [the Kingdom agenda] involves an invasion into the inward parts of man's soul, capturing his heart and mind for the purposes of God" (Munroe 140).

The Anointed One, Christ, priest after the order of Melchizedek, "Having neither beginning of days nor end of life" (Hebrews 7:3), came to fulfill the order of Jewish customs and laws. "For the priesthood being changed, of necessity there is also a change of the law" (Hebrews 7:12). However, Jesus did not seek to change the outward man with his customs, practices, and religious mandates. He came to change people's minds and the way they were living in the hope that they would repent and change the way they were religiously programmed to go which avoided a consecrated life. When Jesus began His Galilean ministry after being tempted in the wilderness by Satan—God's enemy—He proclaimed: "Repent, for the kingdom of heaven is at hand" (Matthew 4:17).

This new order, the Kingdom of God, would supernaturally transform the way in which the consciousness of man would be brought into spiritual alignment with the consciousness of God, bringing glory and exaltation to God, the Father of light. However, mankind had to change his mind—his way of thinking—from the way he had been religiously and culturally taught in order to enter in and take part in this kingdom era. By changing the mindset of the people of His day, Jesus would inevitably bring a new awareness of God's perception of life and purpose for His people. They then would be able to enjoy and benefit from being in alignment with the Creator in life, purpose and destiny.

The Kingdom of God is His representative system that

allows man to receive back from the past a life he previously possessed with God in the Garden of Eden, the perfect environment in which God placed the first man (Genesis 2:8). The first man, Adam, and Eve, his wife, were blessed by God. As they walked with God in the garden they were given dominion, power, and authority to rule their environment (Genesis 1:28).

Moses, the prophet who is credited as writing the first five books of the Bible, described in Genesis 1:28: "Then God blessed them, and God said to them, be fruitful and multiply; fill the earth and subdue it; have dominion over the fish of the sea; over the birds of the air, and over every living thing that moves on the earth." The Kingdom of God is the sphere where mankind is equipped by Jesus to live out God's intended destiny (where man is submitted, empowered, and aligned with God and His redemptive plan).

God chose to use the motif of the "Kingdom" as a way to methodologically communicate His voice to the universe through the church (the community of believers). The Kingdom of God and all its components echo who God is and how He responds to those who believe in Him. God's sphere of rulership is a Theocracy, meaning that God is the only Sovereign Head of mankind. Mankind is born from God and given life through the breath of God's Spirit to be as He is—a living, reigning vessel through which God fulfills His plans on the earth (Ephesians 2:10).

God's realm is a spiritual dimension that includes God's family of believers being built up and made complete in Him that they might be acceptable unto God (paraphrased 1 Peter 2:5). The Kingdom of God, with all its spiritual components—

> *The dimension of God's government in the earth is an extension of God's rulership in the heavens.*

testaments (laws), regulations, and celestial weapons—produce a world of its own within and apart from the natural world where life in the body exists. God's spiritual rulership is also extended to rulership in the heavens. The dimension of God's government in the earth is an extension of God's rulership in the heavens. Myles Munroe, author and Bahamian pastor, in his book *Rediscovering the Kingdom* explains: "God called the invisible realm or domain heaven and thus He became the King over the domain, heaven." The Kingdom of God is therefore viewed by contemporary theologians as a model or prototype of the system of God that is beyond the earth's scope (Munroe 24).

The sovereign dominion of God as a movement is underway and every believer that sees it and presses toward it will join into a corporate destiny that God intended. God is not doing a new thing, but has completed His plan and is awaiting every believer to join in His plan of freedom for this age. The world where God rules inherently possesses within itself the mind of God that moves the universe toward eternal completion. "It is the power of God working through us that will bring about the manifestation or revealing of His

Kingdom" (Charles 13).

The Kingdom is unraveled in a paradigm-shifting facet: A revolution of the consciousness. The spiritual government of God is a Kingdom of consciousness to which the believer has

> The Kingdom is unraveled in a paradigm-shifting facet: A revolution of the consciousness.

to be awakened. God's Kingdom is an awakening of the consciousness of the believer to know that this Kingdom does exist. Concurrently, this awakening also juxtaposes an epiphany of the true identity and purpose of every believer who houses the mind of God within himself.

Contemporary theologians and biblical teachers have given rise to the sphere where God reigns in a physical and social formation (Munroe 44, 45). The king, his domain, and all the strata of theological-political existence in God's Kingdom are the primary focus in the twenty-first century. This theological quest is the dominating motif prevalent in the Body of Christ. This current Kingdom of God theology is the socio-cultural concept for the Kingdom.

This examination will locate the believer within the full spectrum of this huge world of the God's realm of rulership, the Kingdom of God coming to the individual believer within a personal world. If the influence of God's authority is within the believer then the scope of life of the mindset of God starts with the believer and expands to the uttermost universe.

For example, before Jesus ascended to heaven He admonished His disciples to preach the gospel to all nations (paraphrased Acts 1:8). With the individual's consciousness awakened this spiritual realization goes to the end of the earth to reach and impact all mankind.

THE KINGDOM OF GOD AS THE SYSTEM OF GOD

According to *Webster's College Dictionary*, a system is "an ordered and comprehensive assemblage of facts, principles, doctrines, or the like in a particular field; a coordinated body of methods or a scheme or plan of procedure." A system is also having, showing, or involving a method or plan. God had a plan when He established His Kingdom and created His children who would follow after Him and reflect His glory.

As author Myles Munroe exclaimed in his book, *Rediscovering the Kingdom*, "This Kingdom is a [righteous] state government with all of the characteristics of a state" (Munroe 64). Also, according to this author, a kingdom is made up of several components: a monarch or king, land or territory to be ruled over, a covenant, citizenry, organic law initiated by the ruling king or his representatives, benefits for citizens, a code of ethics, a military, a commonwealth, and culture.

As Jesus continued His teachings on devotion to God, the disciple Matthew recorded in his gospel: "Seek first the Kingdom of God and his righteousness and all these things shall be added unto you" (Matthew 6:33). The dimension where God is ruler is the domain or realm where there is

superior title and absolute ownership. It is the domain of the king with his laws, rules, regulations, benefits, constitution, governance, and structure. In addition, the Kingdom presupposes a predefined way of living and a predefined method of existing. It also rests on the concept of God's intended life for every person who participates in His kingdom.

THE MONARCH

A monarch or king is the chief ruler of the kingdom. All established law and authority flow from the king to the participants in the kingdom. It is through the king that the kingdom derives its power and direction. "The king is the embodiment of the kingdom, representing its glory and nature" (Munroe 65). The monarch is one who reigns over a territory usually for a life time and the ruler also gains this position through hereditary rights. The king is the absolute and sole ruler; he is sovereign. He is the supreme commander and the preeminent royalty.

Some of the symbols of the king's office include the crown and the scepter. The crown is the head ornament that symbolizes the highest rank in social and political power. The crown represents the king's reigning sovereignty. The scepter, another piece of royal regalia, is an ornamental staff held by the monarch. It represents the authority and imperial power of the king. The scepter is also used to symbolically extend the grace and favor by the king.

For instance, in 465 B.C. during the time of Esther, Queen of the Persian Empire during the reign of King Ahasuerus, the Jews were under severe threat of annihilation. Queen Esther, who had not been summoned by the king, risked her life and entered his inner court in order to save her people, the Jews. The king extended his golden scepter, offering her entrance and favor instead of death. She touched the top of the scepter, gratefully acknowledging her acceptance of his favor (paraphrased Esther 5:2). With the symbols of power, the king reigns with all authority in his realm.

THE DOMAIN

Domain means, according to *Webster's College Dictionary*, "the territory governed by a single ruler or government." The domain is the land or territory in which the king rules. This is the place or sphere of influence of the king's realm. This realm is the boundary and limitation of the king's jurisdiction. The domain associated with a kingdom usually signifies the accumulated wealth of the king, which includes people, property, and land. The king utilizes his power to exercise full authority and to reign as sovereign within his territory (Munroe 64).

The domain is the realm of the king that is guarded and protected as his estate (property and possessions). The territory over which the king exercises control becomes his realm. The domain of the king is the real estate owned directly by the sovereign. The king's domain is equal to his kingdom, his dimension of influence, and his area of control and power. Concerning domain, the greater the monarch's territory, the greater his realm of control and rulership.

THE COVENANT

The king's covenant is his written words to the citizens of his kingdom. The covenant or testament of the king establishes his relationship with the citizens and serves as an oath of allegiance between him and the people under his authority or rulership (Munroe 65). The covenant expresses the king's will as well as his benefits toward those that follow his decrees. This constitution establishes the king's mind toward all within his domain.

The covenant is also a binding agreement or a formal contract between parties. It is a declaration that one will or will not do a certain act. It is a pledge, an oath, a moral obligation. Some have suggested that the root meaning of the word covenant means "to cut" as in a blood covenant between Abraham and God. God promised Abraham that his descendents would multiple and inherit the land of Israel. Because the animals that God requested Abraham to bring to Him to solidify the covenant were cut in two, the covenant was said to have been made or "cut" between God and Abraham (paraphrased Genesis 15:10). Therefore, the covenant between the sovereign and the citizens is the agreement or contract between the two, assuring obligations are met and reciprocated.

THE CITIZENS

The citizens of a kingdom are those willing to follow the mandate of the ruler in his kingdom. As a result, the citizens live under the laws and sovereignty of the king as well as receive the protection and privilege granted by the king. "The number one goal of a citizen of a kingdom is to submit to the king, seeking only to remain in right standing with him" (Munroe 65). It is the safety of the citizen to work for the king and seek his good. The king has the authority to promote or demote, to permit life or to allow death. It is in the best interest of the citizen first to please the king at every opportunity or in every motive.

Citizens are the residents and civilians of a territory or realm in which a king rules, members of a community with duties associated with membership. The obligations of citizens always center on loyalty and allegiance. Residents are expected to be devoted to the king, adhering to the laws established by him. Abiding by laws the king has established maintains order and provides civil rest for the citizens. Breaking the law of any realm may lead to civil unrest and rebellion against the king and his administration. Law-abiding citizens can be reassured of the king's protection and care.

THE LAW

"The law constitutes the standards and principles established by the king himself, by which his kingdom will function and be administered" (Munroe 65). The fundamental administration and organization of the kingdom rest on established laws. The laws are irrevocable and unchangeable once set in place by the king. He is then bound by the laws that he made. Therefore, the king's word becomes officially the law of the kingdom (Munroe 66).

Laws are the body of rules that govern the affairs of a territory or community and are enforced by legal authority. These rules of conduct are based on morality and order. Laws must be obeyed and followed by citizens. If violated, citizens are subject to sanctions or legal consequences. Laws are the way of life for a community. In God's Kingdom, His laws are the body of precepts held to express His divine will.

THE BENEFITS

In a kingdom, residents experience certain benefits of citizenship. One primary benefit is security; protection granted by the king. In addition, citizens have access to the wealth of the kingdom providing certain laws are kept. They are able to receive the wealth that the kingdom designates to each one. Whatever the need, under the sovereign rule of the king, the citizens are cared for by him (Munroe 66).

In a kingdom, privileges are lavished on faithful and loyal citizens. Citizens are protected and the king is personally responsible for all his citizens. Citizens can be appointed by the king to serve in leadership capacities within the kingdom.

When the king recognizes a loyal and faithful citizen, he can bestow delegated authority to that citizen to serve the king's plans. Citizens also have the right or privilege of working and serving in the kingdom. Citizens can serve in any capacity according to their personal skills and talents to further advance the kingdom's mandate.

THE CODE OF ETHICS

The code of ethics for a kingdom includes the predetermined standard of behavior that the king expects from those under his authority. Each citizen is expected to comply with the king's mandates, which reflect personally upon the king's reputation. The code of ethics is not only for the kingdom itself, but also for the benefit of the citizenry. "This code includes moral standards, social relationships, personal conduct, attitude, attire, and manner of life" (Munroe 66).

The system of moral principles is usually established by the king. These principles reflect values relating to the moral conduct of the citizens. Because the moral principles of the citizens distinguish them from citizens of other kingdoms, ethics are an important part of life for the citizens as well as the kingdom they represent. In the Kingdom of God, citizens are said to be known by the love they show to one another. Jesus expressed this in the Gospel of John: "A new commandment I give to you, that you love one another; as I have loved you, that you also love one another. By this all will know that you are My disciples, if you have love for one another" (John 13:35).

THE MILITARY

An important component of a kingdom is the establishment of a military. The military is directed by the chief officer, the king, to protect and secure his realm and to obey his every command. The military component of the Kingdom of God includes God's army of angelic hosts (Matthew 26:53). Citizens of the Kingdom of God have the benefit of protection and security through God's dictates to His military organization, the angelic hosts.

God's military not only protects his citizens, but also delivers His messages to His citizens (through the angels that God commands.) For example, when Daniel, an administrator of King Cyrus of Persia, prayed and fasted for twenty-one days for an answer from God, God sent a heavenly messenger, an angel, to interpret Daniel's vision (paraphrased Daniel 10:1-12). Angels also are used by God to direct the steps of His people and lead them into His prepared way (Exodus 23:20). Angels are the military servants of the King and bring aid to God's people.

The Commonwealth

The commonwealth of the kingdom is equal to its financial and economic prowess. The commonwealth maintains the sustenance of citizens with all access to its wealth. This is why citizenship is important. "In a kingdom, the term commonwealth is used because the king's desire is that all his citizens share and benefit from the wealth of the kingdom" (Munroe 67). The king is not obligated to care for or release access to the kingdom's wealth to those who are not citizens.

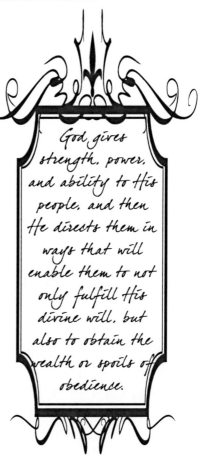

God gives strength, power, and ability to His people, and then He directs them in ways that will enable them to not only fulfill His divine will, but also to obtain the wealth or spoils of obedience.

In a kingdom, the king's desire is for the citizens have financial security through his wealth resources. In the spiritual Kingdom of God, He provides access to His wealth by empowering His people. God gives strength, power, and ability to His people, and then He directs them in ways that will enable them to not only fulfill His divine will, but also to obtain the wealth or spoils of obedience. God instructs through the prophet Isaiah: "If you are willing and obedient, you shall eat the good of the land" (Isaiah 1:19). Therefore, the commonwealth of God is accessed through obedience to His commands, and then His wealth can be enjoyed by His citizens.

SOCIAL CULTURE

Kingdom social culture is played out in the lives and activities of the king and the citizens. "This is the cultural aspect that separates and distinguishes the kingdom from all others around it" (Munroe 67). The culture of the kingdom is the setting or the environment produced by the behavior and mentality of the citizens and their king. All the components of the kingdom's sphere are summed up in its culture; its way of life.

The social culture is the atmosphere created by the lifestyle of the citizens of a kingdom. The culture of the kingdom is evident in the daily activities and relationships established by the citizens as they reflect the king's demeanor in their lives. The essence of the king is known through the behavior and conduct of his citizens. As citizens mature into the culture of a kingdom, they should develop more and more to be like their king. Therefore, the nature of the king is mirrored by the manner and character of the citizens.

Understanding Conciouness and its Types

If the domain of God is a consciousness of the Kingdom of God, then what is consciousness in general? Because of its complexity, consciousness defies simple definition. *Webster's College Dictionary* defines consciousness as the state of being conscious or aware. Consciousness is the activity of the mind and senses that awaken one to life. Internal knowledge is having awareness of something for what it is. It has been defined loosely as "a constellation of attributes of mind such as subjectivity, self-awareness, the power of perception and senses, and the ability to perceive a relationship between oneself and one's environment" (Costello 289). In his book, *The Spectrum of Consciousness*, Ken Wilber explains:

> Consciousness has been defined from a more biological and casual perspective as the act of autonomously altering attentional and computational effort, usually with the goal of obtaining, retaining, or maximizing specific

parameters (food, a safe environment, family, mates).

Consciousness may involve one's thoughts. Thoughts are patterns of thinking or processes whereby thoughts are focused into a particular mindset. Beliefs and opinions, which are the manifestations of thought processes, first form as ideas in the mind. Also, consciousness may involve an awareness of one's self. To be perceptive of self includes understanding how one thinks, how one processes information, and how one judges ethical situations. Consciousness of self is an attribute of the human mind. Consciousness is a point of view or the existence of something similar (Wilbur 118). Therefore, consciousness cannot be confused with perception. It is not the same as cognition (which is a defined process of awareness), and should be sharply distinguished from it. In common parlance, consciousness denotes being awake and responsive to environment in contrast to being asleep or in a coma.

ETYMOLOGY OF CONSCIOUSNESS

The word "consciousness," as derived from Latin *conscientia*, primarily means moral conscience. In the literal sense, *conscientia* (or "con scientia") means knowledge, that is, shared knowledge. Here *conscientia* denotes the knowledge a witness has of an act of someone else.

In Christian theology, conscience stands for moral principles upon which actions and intentions are founded and which are fully known only to God (Musser and Price 215). In the contemporary sense of the word, consciousness is associated with the idea of a personal identity, which is assured by the repeated principle of self. The sense of right and wrong is the power of knowing one's own thoughts and actions and the perception of what passes in one's own mind. Ethics, therefore, according to the contemporary use of the word, reside in the mind. According to the author Jaegwon Kim in his book, *Philosophy of the Mind*:

> Because humans express their conscious states using language, it is tempting to equate language abilities and consciousness. There are, however, speechless humans (infants, feral or unlearned children, aphasics, and severe forms of autism), to whom consciousness is attributed despite language lost or not yet acquired. Language alone does not contribute to the fundamental existence of consciousness.

EXPLORING CONSCIOUSNESS

Having a concept of something means nothing until the reality of that concept is manifested. Intimate knowledge is not mere mental assent, but is moving beyond impressions and becoming one with the awareness of the idea.

For instance, the generation that surrounded Christ had a concept of the Kingdom of God. For generations they had studied, lived, and waited for the reality of the Messiah to be manifested. However, when Jesus walked among them, He taught that "the Kingdom of God is already within you" (Luke 17:21 Amplified). There had to be an awakening and a revelation of the Kingdom of God before the Jewish people could grasp what Jesus was saying. They believed that God's physical Kingdom would come and would overthrow the Roman government during the Roman conquest of Jerusalem (paraphrased Acts 1:6 NKJV). The Romans conquered

Jerusalem in first century BCE and Jerusalem became a province of the Roman Empire ruled by Roman procurators and the Herodian Dynasty. The Jews rebelled against Rome, unsuccessfully, in 66 C.E. In 70 C.E., the Jews experienced the destruction of Jerusalem including Herod's Temple. Much of the population was enslaved or killed (Tenney 103).

Jesus was not teaching about a physical place, but a spiritual and mental Kingdom of God, a coup d'etat in the consciousness, a revolution of mindset.

However, Jesus was not teaching about a physical place, but a spiritual and mental Kingdom of God, a coup d'état in the consciousness, a revolution of mindset. Jesus explained that the Kingdom of God was not just a concept, but a divine revelation of God's thoughts, ideas, methods, and manners; God's culture (Tenney 153). In essence, Jesus asked people to take their traditional way of thinking about the Law of Moses and the prophets and transpose them into the foundation of how God viewed the world, how God made decisions, how God reacted and responded, and how God related to them. Jesus was instructing the people to change their outlook and allow God's way of thinking to supplant what they had known prior to His coming to them. He desired that the people accept this revolutionary change within their mindset.

This transposition could not happen until there was a change in the mind and heart of the people. As recorded by the Apostle John, one of Jesus' close disciples: "Unless you are born again, you cannot see the Kingdom of God" (John 3:3). The Greek word translated "again" can also be rendered "from above." *According to the Greek-English Lexicon of the New Testament* by Carl Grimm, to be born again means to have a spiritual birth from above. Romans 10:10 explains being born again: "That if you confess with your mouth the Lord Jesus and believe in your heart that God has raised Him [Jesus] from the dead, you will be saved." One has to have the viewpoint of heaven extended into his consciousness in order to see God's ways, thoughts, and intentions. There has to be a revelation of who God is in the mind of man in order for him to walk in the mandate of God's Kingdom.

There has to be a revelation of who God is in the mind of man in order for him to walk in the mandate of God's Kingdom.

Consciousness is not a static state; a stationary position showing little or no change. According to *Webster's College*

Dictionary, it is a dynamic process that one has been made aware of and experienced. The believer is constantly being made aware of different Kingdom activities (from local and national soul-winning campaigns to teaching biblical principles, to building hospitals around the world, to being a voice for the homeless and impoverished, to renewing the mind in certain areas, to pursuing the wisdom of God in important decisions), while simultaneously experiencing other Kingdom activities, sometimes within the same span of time. It is a changing, dynamic state of awareness that is constantly on-going in the heart and mind of the believer. For the sake of this investigation, consciousness is not just psychological, mental, or biological, but is a state of awakened focus on God and His undergirding truths.

WORLD CONSCIOUSNESS

COMPETING CONSCIOUSNESSES

Many different types of consciousness compete with the focused consciousness that directs mankind back to the program of reconciliation with the Creator. This program of reconciliation leads man to the focus of the world of God, the Creator, that conforms him to the image of Jesus Christ (paraphrased Romans 8:29). In 56 A.D., the Apostle Paul wrote to the Roman church: "For whom He [God] foreknew He also predestined to be conformed to the image of His Son, that He might be the first born among many brethren" (Romans 8:29). God's plan, therefore, is that man "thinks" like His Son, Jesus Christ. The word "conform" in *Strong's Exhaustive Concordance of the Bible* is, in the Greek, *summorphos*. *Summorphos* is to make of like form with another person or thing; to render like; to assimilate (Strong 238). God's plan is that the thinking of man conforms to the thinking of Christ.

God's plan is that the thinking of man conforms to the thinking of Christ.

God did not only create the human race, but He purposed that His creation ultimately "be" like Christ—to think like Him and implement God's plans as Jesus did.

However, many people are socialized and indoctrinated with a world consciousness that focuses on the world's systems and on the functionality of how mankind, without the true God, thinks. This system not only opposes the thinking of Christ, but is detrimentally antithetical to the nature of Christ. These competing world entities propagate against God's program because man has taken a humanistic, secular worldview. Man's worldview is about self and is driven by a desire to serve self at the cost of annihilating masses of people in the process. In the modern day, human culture utilizes systems and structures to make normal or to legitimize its selfish reign of terror. These systems and structures can be summed up in seven world systems.

These seven world systems include: religion, economy, education, healthcare, legal, military, and government. Each system establishes its own guidelines for propaganda in asserting power over the people under its sphere of influence.

These systems, when combined as one, make up a person's worldview or global view. They are ancient institutions built on a system of belief or consciousness that upholds their worldly structure.

Without the populous legitimizing and giving credence to

these systems they would not survive. For the most part, however, they are accepted and looked upon as "gods" in some cases. Whatever these societal structures do, they are generally not questioned or challenged by the masses. But there are revolutionary heroes who have fought and won against these age-old entities.

For example, Nelson Mandela became South Africa's first black president. In 1994, former President Mandela won the first fully representative democratic presidential election even in the hostile atmosphere of apartheid. As an anti-apartheid activist, Mandela fought against a system that economically and politically subjugated the masses of indigenous black South Africans and won ("Nelson Mandela." *Wikipedia, the Free Encyclopedia*).

Also, as England in the 18th century continued political and economic demands including taxation of the colonists in America, unrest soon moved the immigrants to action (Elson 220). In 1765, the Founding Fathers of America heroically led the American Revolution against Mother England. Seven brave men—George Washington, Thomas Jefferson, John Adams, James Madison, Alexander Hamilton, John Hancock, and Benjamin Franklin—banded together with other colonists and risked their lives for the sake of political, social, and religious freedom. They not only helped solidify victory over England; they authored the Declaration of Independence, the United States Constitution, and the Bill of Rights (Elson 222).

Moreover, the legacy of these historic documents is commemorated in countries all over the world. They are viewed as significant treatises helping to guide nations to more humane treatment of their citizens.

Far too many cultures, however, have not fought against institutional world systems and have suffered the consequences of the inactivity of the reluctant. It is up to believers in God's systems who have the mandate to think outside these institutions and challenge their moral and ethical agendas. By utilizing Kingdom of God awareness, believers have the ability to produce a lasting impact on the world.

The one system that far exceeds the others in mass destruction of the human ability to see the true God is national, institutionalized religion. This is the most insidious of the world systems because religious consciousness, in its secularized form, disguises itself as "consciousness" of God in the world.

This is the form of church that is a national institution with its own self-appointed traditions and man-made concepts of God. Furthermore, through religious regulations, it uses power to keep believers in a place of docility and servility. The institutional church has its own opinions about God, human choice, politics, and all the other grand issues of life. This religious entity seeks its own ways and not the ways of the true God. This mindset is completely contradictory to scriptural truth emanating from Philippians 3:9 which admonished: "Not having my own righteousness, which is from the law, but that which is through faith in Christ, the righteousness which is from God by faith."

The existence and development of world systems stretch back five thousand years, to at least 3000 B.C. (Halsall. "Development of a World Economic System"). The world's systems operate out of an institution of mankind's policies, dogmas, theories, and experiences. These institutions all have their own voices that dictate life, culture, and the thoughts of citizenry. The world's systems intrinsically and ideologically propagate control and advance national and geographical agendas.

As mentioned previously, there are seven entities that make up the totality of the world's consciousness: economic, government, military, legal, healthcare, educational, and religious systems.

ECONOMIC WORLD SYSTEM

The American historian Immanuel Wallerstein developed the concept of a world system as the globally expanding economic unit united by a network of trade and financial coalitions. By definition, a world system is any historical social system of interdependent parts that form a bounded structure and operate according to distinct rules (*Webster's College Dictionary*). The modern world economy is a world system larger than any jurisdictionally defined political unit and the basic linkage between its parts is economic. The world system of economics is thought of by economists and political sociologists as "the connection that cements all the rest of the world systems" (Denemark 4). The world economic system is by far the axis on which all other world's systems turn.

There are three economic domains that are the certainty of national superiority in the sphere of world economic power: industrial production, commerce, and finance. As explained in the article, "Development of a World Economic System," domination in agro-industrial productive efficiency leads to dominance in commercial distribution of world trade (Halsall). Commercial primacy leads in turn to control of the financial sectors of banking and investment. Having economic advantage leads to political power. When producers in a given entity undersell those in another, over time the transformation of production advantage can become a commercial advantage creating dominance in the financial arena. These combined advantages translate into economic supremacy, operating primarily through the world market.

The more money accumulated or the more money within a system, the more nations strive to possess the benefits of its inherent power. In his book, The Moral Consequences of Economic Growth, Harvard University economics professor Benjamin Friedman comments: "Economic growth has become the secular religion of advancing industrial societies" (Friedman 15). This process is apparent when materialism has replaced community and insatiable appetite has replaced peace and contentment. As Jesus, in His earthly ministry, explained to His disciples and the multitude as recorded in Matthew 6:24: "No one can serve two masters; for either he will hate the one and love the other or else he will stand by and be loyal to the one and despise the other. You cannot serve God and mammon" (NKJV).

According to *Strong's Exhaustive Concordance of the Bible*, mammon is interpreted as "wealth personified and avarice deified [or worshipped]" (Strong 156). Mammon is a system that encourages the worship of the false god of riches and avarice; it is an object of veneration and greedy pursuit. The essence of mammon mirrors the mindset of greed. It is the self-centered focus on ambitions, desires, and aspirations for personal gain.

For example, in 2001 a multi-billion-dollar American

Energy Company, Enron, according to the report "Enron Scandal At-A-Glance" by BBC News World Edition, August 22, 2002, filed for bankruptcy because of corporate fraud; at that time, the largest bankruptcy filing in American history. Although this company was the "seventh largest American company with 21,000 employees in forty countries," the firm was embroiled in an elaborate scam of greed and deception. Enron was reported to have lied about profits, concealed debts, and committed fraud and money laundering. After the company's stock plummeted to junk status in 2001, meaning it became worthless on the stock exchange, investigation into the unscrupulous dealings of the firm's executives ensued. The outcome was that thousands of people lost their jobs and billions of dollars in employee pensions.

A noted witness against Enron executives brought to trial was mysteriously found dead in a London park before his could testify (Barnhart. "The Collapse of Enron"). The aftermath of this disparagement included twenty-four guilty pleas, prison convictions, nineteen counts of securities and wire fraud conviction, and stockholders' loss of approximately $11 billion ("Enron Scandal At-A-Glance").

The dishonorable practices of company executives affected not only the corporate industry, but also thousands of American homes. Enron's employees relied on the company for income to support their families and retirement benefits that are now dissolved. After having invested heavily in Enron's now worthless stock, many employees became hopeless and despondent ("Enron Scandal At-A-Glance," BBC News. August, 2002).

Other market scandals followed, spurred by deception,

unethical corporate practices, and fraudulent behavior—United States banking and mortgage systems, AIG Insurance, WorldCom, and many more businesses. One of the largest accounting firms in the world, Arthur Andersen, dissolved amid scandal. Repercussions from these companies' finagling included court convictions, bankruptcies, and government-subsidized financial bailouts. "These conglomerates, through their base financial practices," some political experts surmise, "have initiated the worse economic recession since the Great Depression of the 1930's" ("Enron Scandal At-A-Glance," BBC News, August 2002). As a result, according to the United States Bureau of Labor Statistics, in May 2009, the national unemployment rate reached 9.4%, the highest ever on record at that time.

The New York Times reported an estimated $12.2 trillion promise that the United States government made to rescue and fund the struggling financial system ("Adding up the Government's Bailout Tab," *The New York Times*, February 2009). A government bailout is a government-funded cash infusion into a failing business or an entire market sector. It is the act of giving capital to a company in danger of failing in an attempt to save it from bankruptcy, insolvency, or total liquidation and ruin (Jesse Nankin, "History of U. S. Government Bailouts"). The world reverberated with the ghastly effects of the faltering economic plight of the American economy.

The entire country of Iceland faced national bankruptcy because of its inability to pay its foreign debt, according to reporter Eric Pfanner of *The New York Times* newspaper on October 2008. His article, "Iceland Is All but Officially Bankrupt," explained that the Icelandic government shut down the stock market in late 2008 because of the "debt-fueled binge by the country's banks, businesses, and private citizens." The currency of the country froze and came to a complete halt. Citizens were fearful and angry as they experienced the loss of their homes, life savings, and confidence in the financial system.

Economic supremacy in the world system could possibly wield far-reaching implications over the acceptable practices of humankind including family life, aspirations, morality, and

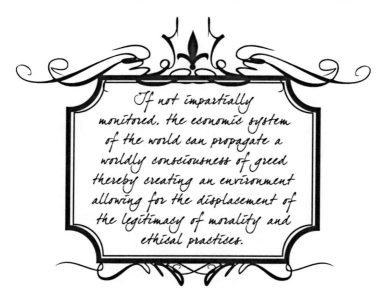

If not impartially monitored, the economic system of the world can propagate a worldly consciousness of greed thereby creating an environment allowing for the displacement of the legitimacy of morality and ethical practices.

normative social behavior. The economic system of a society has the propensity to influence what has value and what does not. It has the potential to dictate what an individual should strive for and what he should possess. If not impartially monitored, the economic system of the world can propagate a worldly consciousness of greed thereby creating an environment allowing for the displacement of the legitimacy of morality and ethical practices. The economic world system has

the ability to be controlled by a system of psychology that inspires lust for money and material possessions in the name of self-exaltation. In this system, most cannot continue to pay the price for their lust for more. Often this lust leads to insurmountable debt, stress, and bondage. Slavery, in essence, according to the teachings of Jesus (paraphrased Romans 6:16), is whatever one submits himself to.

KINGDOM OF GOD CONSCIOUSNESS FOR ECONOMICS

Kingdom of God consciousness regarding economics is established on the regulations of God, who admonishes believers that they should have no other God before Him. In any life or culture where the spirit of Mammon is the primary focus, or the activity of life is overcome by the desire to have, the god of Mammon is prince over that entity. God has an agenda in His Kingdom that all believers must understand. This divine agenda is such that true Kingdom riches have a purpose to further the Kingdom of God through service, support, and restoration. Wealth and riches the way God intended manifest through divine processes that cleanse the character, mature the mind, and glorify the living God.

An understanding of Kingdom economics usually begins with being taught God's Word. In the process, God becomes known or revealed to the believer. The key to this level is to know and understand that God, according to His infinite riches, is that source for whatever is needed. The scripture, in Philippians 4:19, states: "And my God shall supply all your need according to His riches in glory by Christ Jesus." The consciousness of God's revealed character as Provider is explained in 2 Corinthians 9:8: "And God is able to make all grace abound toward you that you, always having all sufficiency in all things, may have an abundance for every good work." One does not have to lust for what he already has. If God has supplied everything then the question of having any human need should be answered. God has the responsibility of furnishing all things necessary to sustained life. This is one of the promises of God to those that belong to Him.

After this process of understanding God through witnessing His provision, God often moves the believer toward maturing in the ability to possess abundance. In the first five books of the Bible, the Pentateuch, which consists of the books of Genesis, Exodus, Leviticus, Numbers and Deuteronomy, Moses, the servant of God, admonished the Hebrew people to remember the Lord, for it was God who gave the ability to get wealth in order to establish His promises to the whole earth (Deuteronomy 8:18).

The abilities God gives are power, strength, and capacity in mind and spirit (Psalm 68:35 and 2 Timothy 1:7). God renders all the raw materials—talents, skills, and the spiritual weapons of prayer and His Word—to empower every believer to possess necessary resources for the advancement of His Kingdom plan.

The wealth mentioned in Deuteronomy 8:18 denote more than just everyday needs being supplied. As stated in the article, "What Happened to Our Abundance?" by pastor and teacher Michael Smith of Jacksonville, FL, "Wealth indicates a surplus, plentiful amount, and any extra after basic essentials are fulfilled." The extra or the surplus goes to serve others and to maintain a momentous thrust for the Kingdom agenda. At this stage of spiritually maturing, the resources exceed all of life's requirements and basic needs. However, wealth poses a slight dilemma to every believer. Can one hold the balance that wealth requires? Can the believer be disciplined enough to take care of life's basics, create provisions for others, and fund Kingdom programs? Believers, in this stage of wealth-garnering must be obedient and disciplined in order to maintain their position and continually move into the next dimension of God's wealth system.

Through the practice of Godly humility—humbling oneself to the will and purposes of God—Solomon, King of Israel (reigning from 970-930 B.C.) was established by God as the richest man in the world (Hayford 488). During his early rule as king of a united Israel, Solomon was given a dream where God encouraged him to ask for whatever he wanted. Solomon answered:

> Now, O Lord my God, You have made Your servant king instead of my father David, but I am a little child; I do not know how to go out or come in. And Your servant is in the midst of your people, too numerous to be numbered or counted. Therefore give to Your servant an understanding heart to judge your people, that I may discern between good and evil. For who is able to judge this great people of Yours? (1 Kings 3:7-9).

God answered Solomon in a great and pleasing way:

> Because you have asked this thing, and have not asked long life for yourself, nor have asked for riches for yourself, nor have asked the life of your enemies, but have asked for yourself understanding to discern justice, behold, I have done according to your words; see, I have given you a wise and understanding heart, so that there has not been anyone like you before you, nor shall any

like you arise after you. And I have also given you what you have not asked: both riches and honor, so that there shall not be anyone like you among the kings all your days (1 Kings 3:11-13).

In *Webster's College Dictionary*, the meaning of the word humility is a modest opinion of one's own importance or rank. Even as king over one of the world's greatest nations of the Mediterranean at that time, Solomon humbled himself before the God he worshipped and asked for an understanding heart—a hearing heart—to rightly judge the nation of God's people. By stating that he was a little child, Solomon was not speaking of chronological years. He admitted his inexperience in the weighty matters of judging a kingdom of people (Hayford, 490).

The virtue of humility is important in the Kingdom of God in that it helps the believer trust in God instead of trusting his own ingenuity for wealth and riches. Humility in the Greek "describes a person who is devoid of all arrogance and self-exaltation—a person who is willingly submitted to God and His will" (Strong 247). In his epistle, the Apostle Peter proclaimed: "Therefore humble yourselves under the mighty hand of God, that He may exalt you in due time" (1 Peter 5:6). The believer has to bring himself low and be "under" God's hand, trusting Him in obedient submission, in order to be exalted by God. With humility to God comes the promise of exaltation or increase in rank, honor, and power.

When he spoke what he desired—to judge rightly—Solomon elevated the will of God and the needs of his nation above his own desires. He demonstrated excellent selflessness in his choice of petitions to the Creator, that God meet the civic needs (the social order) of his young nation. Beyond human desires to defeat surrounding armies, to establish his political agenda, or to build a grand monument to himself, Solomon thought of his people first and asked God to grant him wisdom to hear right instructions and to judge the people fairly.

Solomon's answer pleased and delighted God (paraphrased 1 Kings 3:10), and God entrusted Solomon with great wisdom. People from other countries heard about Solomon's divine wisdom and traveled long distances hear his wisdom (paraphrased 1 Kings 4:30; 1 Kings 4:34).

Not only did God grant Solomon uncommon, renowned wisdom, but He also rendered to him what he did not request—great riches (paraphrased 1 Kings 13). In the article "International Trade: A Source of Solomon's Wealth," the author creates a picture of what the king's wealthy age typified:

> Solomon's yearly based revenues amounted to 50,000 pounds of gold, not counting the gold he received as gifts and tributes. Having access to this vast wealth, Solomon built a magnificent temple for God and a palace complex for himself in Jerusalem. He covered the inside walls and even the floors of the temple with pure gold. Solomon had a large throne of ivory overlaid with gold. He provided his guards with hundredsof golden ceremonial shields. His palace dining service included solid gold cups and plates. Nothing was made of silver during Solomon's timebecause it was considered too ordinary. This was literally Israel's golden era.

Solomon was given the notoriety of great wealth and riches by God because he used the principles of humility and trust in

God to lead a great nation in government and civic responsibilities. Solomon abased himself and God elevated him with great glory, riches, and fame as the king also served the people under his authority with wise rulings and righteous judgments. The Queen of Sheba, or the Queen of the South as Jesus referred to her in Matthew 12:42, praised Solomon for his position of honor and humility toward his God: "Blessed be the Lord your God, who delighted in you on the throne of Israel! Because the Lord has loved Israel forever, therefore He has made you king, to do justice and righteousness" (1 Kings 10:9).

Abundance is void without a Kingdom of God purpose or Kingdom of God consciousness. The believer learns to manage the wealth—the extra or surplus—by how he responds to the directives of God. Having little or no consciousness of God's mandates will result in wealth being squandered, or at least misplaced. It takes sagacious strategy to convert the extra or the overflow of material wealth or other entities into a mission-purposed resource system. This is one reason God's system of economics has to be known and clearly understood in the consciousness of His followers. The world system of economics creates unscrupulous ways to devour the extra, but God has need of wealth on the earth to perpetuate His earthly Kingdom design for all generations to come.

Political and Governmental World Systems

The governmental world system is complex. According to the investigative work of Lester Brown in his book, *State of the World*:

> Government is a system of social control under which the right to make laws, the right to enforce them, is vested in

a particular group in society. The basic law determining the form of government is called the constitution, and it may be written, as in the United States, or unwritten, as in Great Britain. Modern governments perform many functions besides the traditional ones of providing internal and external security, order and justice; most are involved in providing welfare services, regulating the economy, and establishing educational systems. The extreme case of government regulation of every aspect of people's lives is totalitarian (Brown 178-179).

Political and governmental world systems hinge on the ability of a nation, country, or government to flex its political influence on the world at large to gain an advantaged position on the political front. The political systems of the world are systems of authoritative rule and these institutions operate to angle themselves for dominance and control to possess power, economic supremacy, and world clout (Charles 185). The structural establishments of government and politics have become the connective framework of commerce, global finance, and technological advancement. These systems set laws, governance, and international policies. Many of these systems of politics and government control world order in as much as they support and back the systems' stances even if the stances are not in the country's best interests.

For instance, according to social economist Angus Maddison, Political systems and governments have been creating laws and policies that affect national economies for centuries, including the reckless monetary policy of Russia in the mid-to-late 1990's contributing to the hyperinflation of that nation to cover its deficit (Maddison 159).

World systems of government and politics seem to undergird their missions with the overarching theme of power and control. Power and control are human vices that, in the end, usually prove disastrous. This point is further illuminated in the area of human action. Politics is derived from the attempt to use power to administrate the communal aspect of life where the ideal of a perpetually changing society must exist. Politics seek to control through creating, enforcing, and legislating life for the populace. Government and politics have created divisive concepts from imperialism, colonization, and Diasporas, to human slavery. All this destruction is propagated in the name of control and dominance leading to power and preeminence on the world stage.

Power and control are human vices that, in the end, usually prove disastrous.

For instance, the political and governmental regime of South Africa—apartheid—relegated black natives to the edges of the society and stripped them of personhood and dignity through the corruption of a nationalized segregation system (Omer-Cooper 169). According to The Kairos Theologians and the *Kairos Document*, reprinted in 1986, the assertion of this political system comes under serious scrutiny as explained:

> The South African apartheid system is one that justifies the status quo with its racism, capitalism and totalitarianism. It blesses injustice, canonizes the will of the powerful and reduces the poor to passivity, obedience

and apathy. This system does this by misusing theological concepts and biblical texts for its own political purposes. The State in its oppression of the people makes use again and again of the name of God. Military chaplains use it to encourage the South African Defense Force, police chaplains use it to strengthen policemen and cabinet ministers use it in their propaganda speeches. But perhaps the most revealing of all is the blasphemous use of God's holy name in the preamble to the new apartheid constitution: In humble submission to Almighty God, who controls the destinies of nations and the history of peoples; who gathered our forebears together from many lands and gave them this their own; who has guided them from generation to generation; who has wondrously delivered them from the dangers that best them (The *Kairos Document* 3,6).

The political system of the world tends to strip a portion of humankind of dignity and personhood for the sake of its own agenda of power and economic advantage. The race of humanity was formulated after the divine nature of God with the abilities to create, produce, and realize personal divine destinies (paraphrased Genesis 1:26, 27). Mankind was created to dominate the earth, not each other. The human race was given the responsibility to manage the resources of the earth, not to control one another. Because men and women are derived from the image and likeness of divinity, nobility and worth are presumed expectations of all races and ethnicities. When the purposes of the human race become misappropriated, domination becomes the rule of the day and individual rights—

Mankind was created to dominate the earth, not each other.

including choosing one's own destiny with dignity–perish. Tyrannical consequences ensue, subjugating peoples in the name of political or governmental order.

The world's system of politics and government answers the question: Who is in charge? These systems exercise authority based on a classification of rules; thus, in its essence, government is composed of systems that have everything to do with rulership. Governmental rulership fundamentally is set up in a hierarchical structure that has to do with the organization of social classes. These social classes involve structures that rule and cause others to be accountable to the ruling body. In this world system of politics and government, the way the systems are constructed creates policies that are inherently biased and contrived because they represent a systemic divergence of peoples where there is constant polarization. Representation is usually designated from the pool of the wealthy and highly influential, thus magnifying such polarization. This process keeps the gap between the governing body and the subjected body perpetually extensive.

The government and the political systems of this world propose to speak for the people at large and operate for the people, but customarily these systems have neither contact nor rapport with the common people other than their constituents, the client representatives. Consequently, this operation begs the question: How can a nation govern a people when the people's desires are not represented? It becomes visibly clear that the world systems of government and politics exist for subjugation and control that perpetuate a position of being the superpower in the world of economic advantage and international dominance.

KINGDOM OF GOD POLITICAL AND GOVERNMENTAL SYSTEM

When there is an atmosphere of chaos and disorder in the government or political systems then chaos and disorder manifest themselves in the other realms of the society. However, in the Kingdom of God, where there is a consciousness of the laws and commands of God—laws that create order, peace, and productivity—there will be an atmosphere of peace and order. As Jesus Christ was fulfilling His earthly ministry, He taught in Matthew 6:33: "But seek first the kingdom of God and his righteousness, and all these things shall be added to you." The righteousness of God is a position of right standing with God and right relationship with each other.

Righteousness is one of the chief attributes of God where its pivotal meaning centers on ethical conduct (paraphrased Leviticus 19:36; Deuteronomy 25:1). Righteousness is an attribute that is also used in a legal sense where the guilty are judged and the guiltless are deemed righteous (Psalm 109:7; Psalm 37:12-16). The righteous are those who trust that they will be vindicated by God (Psalm 37:12-13). One has no peace and no order when not in right standing with God. An awareness of this righteousness or right standing with God presupposes a consciousness of righteousness.

God's political and governmental systems can be summed up expressly from the scriptural text of Luke 10:27: "You shall love the Lord your God with all your heart, with all your soul, with all your strength, and with all your mind, and your neighbor as yourself." God expects the vertical relationship (between He and the believer) and the horizontal relationship (between the believer and others) to be top priority in the believer's life (Hayford 1448). Without this bridge, access to the advantages of God's political and governmental systems is blocked. Some benefits to God's political and governmental systems are peace, order, authority, and right relations with God and humanity.

MILITARY WORLD SYSTEMS

The fundamental role of government is the protection and security of its citizens, national boundaries, and economic interests (Osborne 311). To fulfill this fundamental role necessitates a national defense mechanism—the military or nation-sanctioned armed forces. The world systems concerning the military are another facet of man's ability to construct entities to uphold the quest for power and dominance in the world.

The military in most countries is an outgrowth of the economic and political structure which bestows power and credence to the advancement of their military structure to enforce its policies and laws nationally and internationally; consequently, the government seeks to maintain a monopoly on the use of this military force (Adler 80-81).

The military is an arm of the government employed to

enforce territorial ownership of nations. It may carry out war tactics of delegated power to protect the interests of the state.

The larger and more advanced the armed forces of a nation, the more presence the nation has in the world; the quest for power and preeminence.

The military is an organization authorized to use force, usually including the use of weapons, in defending its country.

Although a military is not limited to nations in and of itself as many private military companies (or PMC's) can be used or "hired" by organizations and figures as security, escorts, or other means of protection when the state's military is unavailable or not trusted (Hickman, "Leading at Sea").

The military is established as a force with the capability to execute the national defense policy created by the government. Implementation of defense strategy requires specific expert knowledge of how a military functions and how it fulfills its roles.

The military is also responsible for translating policy into missions and tasks and expressing them in terms understood by subordinates, generally called military commands:

The military organization makes these commands possible through the effective use of the delegation of authority through rank. Breaking rank and order of authority usually results in immediate dismissal, excommunication, imprisonment, or a combination of these penalties. The command element of the military is often a strong influence on the organizational culture of the forces. As most political and social analysts reasoned: The role of the military today is as central to society as it

ever was (Hickman, "Leading at Sea").

In the world's system of military prowess there seems to be an illusion of security where the military is concerned; the more displaced national pride, the more of a false sense of safety. The *Oxford Essential Dictionary of the U.S. Military* highlights the point that: "Most citizenry look to the military of the country to protect against any hostile forces, therefore, they pride themselves in this area of governance. However, this pride in military strength can have devastating consequences if overly distorted."

For example, under the leadership of the General of Rome, Gaius Julius Caesar, the ancient empire glorified the strength and might of its military proficiency. During his reign, Julius Caesar conquered many lands and gained extensive geographical territory for Rome. This seemingly impenetrable country with its strong military was an iconic superpower in its day until it imploded and became susceptible to invasion (Giovanni Milani-Santarpia, "Julius Caesar"). After Caesar was killed many Roman city-states were divided among his captains. Ancient Roman ruins point to the precarious historical notion of trusting a military and political government created by the vulnerable intellect of human ambition under the guise of governing for the people.

MILITARY CONSCIOUSNESS IN THE KINGDOM OF GOD

It is important to note that the Kingdom of God also has a military for the "securing of its territory and protecting its citizens" (Munroe 66). This military, however, is not structured

like the world's systems of military bureaucracy. The army of God consists of an invisible array of angelic hosts (paraphrased Psalm 103:20-21). God Himself fights on behalf of the believer with invisible, heavenly weapons not of this world (Matthew 14:40-42). At His arrest in Gethsemane during His earthly ministry, Jesus spoke to one of His disciples, Peter, concerning access to God's military rank and file of angelic soldiers: "Or do you think that I cannot now pray to my Father and He will provide Me with more than twelve legions of angels?" (Matthew 26:53).

The God-conscious believer understands that although necessary, the might of a human military regime has limited strength. The believer understands that there is another kind of military far stronger than human might—God's military. The human, natural military that exists to carry out orders from a sometimes corrupt and inhumane government should not be depended upon by law-abiding people. Trust in even a good and civil governmental order is still unwise. The focus of the believer is to understand and know that God has provided security and safety for those who totally trust in Him. He administers protection to believers.

The security system of God involves angels that are supernatural servants and messengers, ministering as protectors of God's chosen people (Hayford 86). In the book of Exodus, an angel was sent to protect Hebrew slaves from the pursuing Egyptian army (paraphrased Exodus 14:19-20). The angel positioned himself behind the people of God to make a protective gap between them and the Egyptians, creating light for them and darkness for the enemy. This allowed the Hebrews to miraculously cross the divided Red

Sea, but administered destruction to Pharaoh, King of Egypt, and his entire army (paraphrased Exodus 14:21-30). God provided protection and security to His people through the use of His angelic hosts. The people of Israel did not have to physically fight the Egyptian army; however, they trusted God and obeyed His commands.

God still protects His people and secures them with His presence (paraphrased Exodus 33:15). The word "presence" in the Hebrew means to face, to regard, to respect, to turn toward something, to pay attention to it (Strong 228). After 400 years of slavery, Moses led the people of Israel out of Egyptian bondage. He said to God that he would not proceed to another place unless God's presence went with them (Exodus 33:15). Moses earnestly desired God's favor, protection, and regard to distinguish the new nation from all the surrounding tribes (Exodus 33:16). Moses surmised that without the presence of God they would not be victorious against their enemies. With God's divine help, Moses and the people of Israel carried out multiple military campaigns against their enemies (paraphrased Numbers Chapter 21).

God's military system is different from the world's. God's military is an invisible, heavenly organization that serves God's will (Hayford 1873). The author of the Epistle of Hebrews comments concerning the heavenly assistance of angels: "Are they not all ministering spirits sent forth to minister for those who will inherit salvation?" (Hebrews 1:14). Angels are continually active today in building up believers in Christ, advancing the ministry of Jesus, and serving the church (Hayford 1873).

The world's military systems are active in protecting their

nation's interests and not God's interests.

> They serve the state in parliamentary agendas that are
> confined to localize benefits and state welfare, at the
> exclusion of the benefits of many of even those within its
> own territory. The world's military organizations have
> power bestowed on them by governments; therefore, the
> military's power can be controlled by the government of
> which it serves ("Military." The *Oxford Essential Dictionary
> of the US Military*).

Their plans, strategies, and priorities can be dictated by personal ambition rather than the common good, leaving many citizens subject to the consequences of biased national programs. God's structure of military exists to carry out His good toward all mankind. Protection, peace, and security are God's salvific plans from the beginning of the human race. Psalm 29:11 declares: "The Lord will give strength to His people; the Lord will bless His people with peace." God desires that all come to Him and His Kingdom to guarantee His provision and rest (paraphrased Matthew 11:28-30).

The world's military forces only operate in the physical, material realm. They train, fight, and strategize based on the five senses and human perception. But in God's military organization the fight is in the supernatural realm, a world not flanked by physical or human limitations. In 2 Kings Chapter 6, Elisha, the prophet, was pursued by the Syrian army for supplying the Syrian enemies with divinely-revealed military intelligence (paraphrased 2 Kings 6:8-12). Elisha's servant, Gehazi, woke to find an entire army surrounding their city. Fearful, he called Elisha. The prophet responded:

Do not fear, for those who are with us are more than those that are with them. And Elijah prayed, and said, Lord, I pray, open his eyes that he may see. Then the Lord opened the eyes of the young man, and he saw. And behold, the mountain was full of horses and chariots of fire all around Elisha" (2 Kings 6:8-17).

Elisha prayed that the servant might be able to see beyond his physical restrictions into another dimension. As the Syrian army approached Elisha, he prayed that they would be struck with blindness. The entire army became blind and Elisha led them to Samaria, to the location of their enemy, Israel. Elisha then prayed that the men's eyes be opened. They could see again and realized they were in enemy territory. Elisha commanded that food and water be given to the Syrian army.

They ate and were sent back to their master, the Syrian King. The Syrian raiders came no more into Israel's territory. Elisha's servant, after his eyes were supernaturally opened, was able to witness the host of angels present to execute God's formidable victory over the Syrian army. God's army, although invisible to men, were ready to do battle in the interest of His people.

The Kingdom-conscious believer must comprehend the strength of God through His military arrangement established as a benefit to all believers. It is a consciousness that has its foundation in trusting God's unfailing protection. The world's system of military security is limited by human-erected structure. It is unable to comprehensively protect. God's system of military enables the believer to go beyond even the natural world to access the supernatural power of the angelic hosts of heaven.

LEGAL WORLD SYSTEM

The legal world system is positioned to create laws, ordinances, and policies that govern the world. Laws differ from nation to nation, country to country, and city to city. The inherent problem with man-constructed laws is that they are established based on what someone "thinks" is right and wrong. These laws are subjective and can change based on who opposes or benefits from them. Human laws are far from error-free.

> Laws are the principles and regulations established by a government or other authority and applicable to a people, whether by legislation or by custom enforced by judicial decision. Laws are the rules of conduct established for a particular community and backed by municipal authorities. Laws regulate expected behavior, as well as dictate acceptable social norms (Clarke 126).

Laws are an arrangement of regulations established and enforced through a set of authoritative organizations, usually governmental institutions. These regulations shape politics, economics, and society in a number of ways, and serve as primary social mediation in relations between people. Legal systems thoroughly develop rights and responsibilities in a variety of ways. The study of law raises complex issues concerning equality, fairness, liberty, and justice.

In a democracy (where the people rule directly or indirectly through elected officials), a core institution consisting of three central branches—judiciary, legislature, and executive—creates and interprets the law (MacMullen 90). These three serve as a check-and-balance system to limit each area of government. Through this process no one branch can become too powerful.

To execute and enforce the law and provide services to the masses, a government's bureaucracy (political administrative procedures), and the military are vital. While all these entities of the state are auxiliaries created and obligated by law, an independent, legal profession and a vibrant civil society inform and support their progress (Osborne 166).

The judiciary branch exists to govern the administration of justice (MacMullen 90). A judiciary is a number of judges mediating disputes to determine outcome. Most countries have systems of appeals courts, answering to a supreme legal authority. In the United States this is the Supreme Court. The judiciary branch of government is bound by the constitutional establishment of the nation.

Congress in the United States and the Houses of Parliament in London represent the legislative branch of government responsible for the formation of laws. By the principle of representative government, citizens of the country vote for politicians to carry out their wishes. According to author Paul Clarke: "Most countries are a bicameral legislature having two separately appointed legislative houses. The upper house is not directly elected, such as the Canadian Senate, which was in turn modeled on the British House of Lords." In the lower house politicians are elected to represent smaller constituencies. Before a bill can be signed into law and become effective it must be passed by a majority of those voting in each house of the legislature. Normally there will be several readings and amendments proposed by the different political factions.

The executive branch serves as government's central

political authority. In a parliamentary system—as with Britain, Italy, Germany, India, and Japan—the executive is known as the cabinet and is composed of members of the legislature. The Prime Minister chooses the executive.

The other executive model is the presidential system—found in France, the United States, and Russia. In the presidential system, the president acts as both head of state and head of government, and has the power to appoint an unelected cabinet ("Democracy").

Within the presidential system, the executive branch is separate from the legislature, to which it is not accountable.

The role of the executive proposes the majority of legislation, and initiates government agenda. In the presidential system, the executive often has the power to veto or reject legislation. The executive branch also is responsible for the management of foreign relations, the military and police, and the bureaucracy—administration marked by hierarchical authority among numerous offices and by fixed procedures (MacMullen 91).

The problematic nature of man-made laws is based on the subjective bias of human opinion. "Manmade laws originate from a disposition of self-preservation" (Charles 151). Laws are developed to protect and secure society from violations against personhood, property, or civil rights. Laws based on the protection of the people of the nation are good; however, when laws only uphold corruption and disregard for human life, the law goes outside its legal purpose (Omer-Cooper 243).

International conflict and world chaos occur when one nation's laws cross the line of the laws of another. Laws in each country pertain to the wellness of that country, but the same laws might not lend themselves to the

The problematic nature of man-made laws is based on the subjective bias of human opinion.

wellbeing of another nation. In that case, the need for compromise becomes apparent. The double standard that this scenario engenders also breeds hostility within the group or nations that might not receive the same beneficial outcome of the law.

> Therefore, the obvious job of any legal system is to sort out how a law will be implemented, under what conditions will the law be executed, and who will benefit or be penalized according to the statues of the law (Baldwin 110).

A wealthy, influential perpetrator might afford expensive, well-prepared legal representation whereas a poorer, less influential perpetrator might not be able to afford the same quality of representation. Which one would more likely be indicted? Statistics show that wealthy perpetrators have a greater chance of beating criminal charges in court because of their ability to hire better legal representation. It does not matter whether or not a crime was committed; that would not be the issue. In any court case, legal representation must deliver substantial evidence, argue the point around the evidence, and make a convincing case for a client in order to have a chance of winning the case.

The legal systems of the world, where laws of justice and equality are in place, especially in North America and Western Europe, base laws on man-made systems of justice. Ambitious, power-seeking politicians and governmental officials try to align themselves with the notion of justice. Justice then becomes relegated to limited thoughts and feelings about personal security and ways to keep and expand economic and political power.

From the legislative branch that creates laws to the judicial and executive branches where justice is administered and superintended, the world's legal systems are yet struggling with the elusive nature of fairly administering justice and establishing non-partisan, impartial politics for citizens.

KINGDOM OF GOD LEGAL CONSCIOUSNESS

The legal consciousness originating from the Kingdom of God lodges on the spiritual position of divine inheritance. Divine inheritance dictates the legal right of every believer to plead justice of their lawlessness through the death on the cross of Jesus Christ, the Savior of mankind. The law of justification says that sins are accounted as though they were never committed because Christ took the sins of the world, being God in flesh, and nailed them to the cross (paraphrased Romans 4:24-25; 5:1). The word justification in the Greek—*dikaioo*—means to render just or innocent, be freed or deemed to be right (Strong 69). This author notes:

> Mankind is declared righteous before God on certain conditions laid down by Him. Justification is the legal

and formal acquittal from guilt by God as Judge; the pronouncement of the sinner as righteous, who believes on the Lord Jesus Christ. Justification is primarily by faith (Strong 69).

"Christ's resurrection specifically obtains [the believer's] justification, which is [his] being declared righteous in God's sight" (Hayford 1694).

Receiving into one's life and heart this sacrificial substitution through Jesus Christ not only rescues man from his fate of death, but delivers him into an eternally-justified life with God as a citizen of heaven (Hayford 1694). The law of justification is the inheritance and benefit of those who are justified by God. The Apostle Paul writes in his pastoral letter to the Corinthian church: "But you were washed, but you were sanctified, but you were justified in the name of the Lord Jesus and by the Spirit of our God" (1 Corinthians 6:11).

The requirements of the written laws of Moses and the prophets were fulfilled through the price of Jesus' blood, His life. When God supernaturally released the Hebrew people out of Egyptian slavery (Exodus 12:42), He intended to develop a nation that would be an example of His exceptional love and holiness to the rest of the world (Exodus 19:4-6). The laws given to Moses on Mount Sinai were the Ten Commandments:

> You shall have no other gods before Me. You shall not make for yourselves a carved image. You shall not take the name of the Lord your God in vain. Remember the Sabbath day to keep it holy. Honor your father and your mother. You shall not murder. You shall not commit

adultery. You shall not steal. You shall not bear false witness against your neighbor. You shall not covet your neighbor's house (Exodus 20:1-17).

These laws God gave to Moses and the nation are the principles constituting the covenant (the promised arrangement) between God and His chosen people. The Ten Commandments are God's rules and guidelines to govern His people in the way of His intended purposes.

The Ten Commandments guided Israel's relationship to God and to each other. With the first four commandments God instructed the people how to serve Him and what was pleasing to Him in terms of a personal relationship. The Creator commanded that they give Him first place in their lives with no other god except Him alone (paraphrased Exodus 20:1). The Children of Israel not only came out of a polytheistic country where the culture worshiped many gods, but they were going to a place—Canaan—where the people ritualistically served and worshipped many foreign gods (Laymon 42). God desired to make the nation a distinguishing example by their adherence to His laws.

The last six commandments pointed toward a selfless relationship with others by beginning with how to treat parents. God instructed the people that parents were to be honored. Honor, in *Webster's College Dictionary*, means "to give credit or high respect; a source of credit or distinction, to praise highly." In a society, the family makes up the foundation of the community. Therefore, understanding the proper role of the family is paramount.

These final commands then referred to one's neighbors,

prohibiting false witness or coveting anything belonging to someone else. They also encompassed relationship to one's community in terms of the prohibition of murder, adultery, and theft. God demonstrated His value of human life by establishing the commandment against murder. Being faithful is a virtue God displayed as He prohibited adultery. Faithfulness carries over into every dimension of life. God's warning against stealing was a precaution against covetousness; deep longing and intense craving for forbidden possessions or the gratifying of sensual desires.

No member of the human race could properly keep all these laws, but they were fulfilled through Jesus Christ. Now, as part of the inheritance, God accounts the substitutional work of Christ to all who believe in Him and they are justified through His death and resurrection. Because all of mankind is unrighteous due to his sin nature, he deserved the judgment of God. However, Jesus Christ paid the penalty for man's unrighteousness by dying on the cross at Calvary as a substitutionary sacrifice to save mankind from eternal separation from God. Therefore, justification is the position of right standing with God through accepting what Jesus did on the cross. In addition, Jesus not only died, but was raised by God to become the eternal Justifier of mankind. In the scriptural text written by the Apostle Paul, he declares: "For all have sinned and come short of the glory of God, being justified freely by His [Christ's] grace through the redemption that is in Christ Jesus" (Romans 3:23-24).

God dispensed the law to a nation of people to show them that they could not keep the law through their own efforts, revealing the need for a savior—Jesus Christ. One of the reasons the law was introduced was to assist people to understand their need for God's divine strategy of giving them a Savior to rescue them from their sin. All the laws of God are legal acts performed and fulfilled on behalf of the believer. Therefore, the law of God requires belief in the justifying work of the Son of God and acceptance of this position of legal grace by faith (paraphrased Galatians 2:16; John 3:15, 16).

There has to be a consciousness of this act of God's grace in the Kingdom of God where the fulfillment of the law has already taken place. Consequently, all that is required of an individual is to believe and accept this work of grace as foundational truth to allow manifestation of its benefits. One must experience walking out this truth in everyday life, but the reality is that the price of this righteous work was paid by Jesus, God's Son.

Therefore, the legal system of God (redemption through Jesus for the forgiveness of sin) was constructed for the benefit of all mankind, not just for a few privileged persons. God's laws are righteous and pure (Psalm 19:8). They can be followed and executed because of the power Jesus gives to live within them. Kingdom consciousness assists in recognizing this truth and appropriating it in life circumstances. Knowledge of the legal aspects of God's Kingdom helps one to please God.

THE WORLD'S SYSTEM OF HEALTHCARE

According to *Webster's College Dictionary,* "healthcare is the prevention, treatment, and management of illness and the preservation of mental and physical well-being through the services offered by the medical and allied health professions."

A healthcare system refers to a country's provision for the

delivery of services for the prevention and treatment of disease and for the promotion of physical and mental well-being (Breslow 20). The healthcare industry incorporates several sectors dedicated to providing services and products exclusively for improving the health of individuals.

The healthcare industry, according to market classifications, includes healthcare equipment and services, pharmaceuticals, biotechnology, and life sciences. The article "Health Care" published by the Bureau of Labor Statistics states:

> According to the International Standard Industrial Classification healthcare generally consists of hospital activities, medical and dental practice activities, and other human health activities, such as nursing homes, psychotherapists, scientific and diagnostic laboratories, occupational therapy, and chiropractic.

The World Health Organization (WHO) is a United Nations agency that coordinates and researches public health around the world.

> Headquartered in Geneva, Switzerland, the agency's mission is the attainment by all peoples of the highest possible level of health. This agency has the daunting task of fighting world-wide diseases, especially infectious diseases and promoting the overall health of all nations. In 1979, having fought smallpox (a viral spot-producing disease capable of causing death) for many years, the organization declared the extinguishment of the disease. Smallpox is the first disease in history to be completely eliminated by human architecture (World Health Organization 2009)

Because healthcare is a system of human design, it brings many economic, moral, legal, and political issues. Dr. W. K. Mariner, in his article, "Rationing Healthcare and the Need for Credible Scarcity," addresses scarcity as a prominent issue in the distribution of public health (American Journal of Public Health, 1993). Although the World Health Organization's mission is that people all over the world have access to the highest level of healthcare, there is yet scarcity in its allocation.

For example, when American President Bill Clinton assumed office in 1993, the number of uninsured Americans was estimated at 40 million; when he left office, in 2001, that number had climbed to around 48 million (United States Department of Labor Statistics 2007). The U.S. healthcare system has become inundated with complications, "red tape," and bureaucracy estimated to be two-to-four-times that of other Western industrialized nations ("Health Care Statistics").

Because of technological and scientific advancements in medicine, unprecedented moral and ethical issues have stormed the healthcare industry. Healthcare professionals and individuals find themselves having to answer questions concerning the meaning of life and death, when and how to turn off artificially life-supporting devices, and how to obtain properly-informed consent for clinical care and research trials. In addition, cloning, stem cell research, and abortion issues continue to take priority in the minds of the concerned world. To most observers, however, the most critical problem of the healthcare system is soaring costs. Even with government-subsidized health insurance (Medicare and Medicaid), healthcare expenditures have increased exponentially from 6% to 9% of the country's gross domestic product (GDP) ("Health Care Statistics"). The GDP is an economic term for the yearly market value of all goods and services of a nation (*Webster's College Dictionary*). Insurmountable healthcare costs have become a reality for millions of Americans as well as for the national economy.

In an effort to control costs, the business-imposed approach of "managed care" appeared as a solution to the problematic nature of healthcare expenditures. In his article, "Missing the Meaning of Healthcare Reform," Lyle Schofield asserts:

> Managed care is the generic term that refers to a large variety of reimbursement plans in which third-party payers attempt to control costs by limiting the utilization of medical services. Examples of such cost-savings strategies include physicians prescribing drugs only on a plan's approved list, mandated preauthorizations before hospitalization or surgery, severe restrictions on the length of time a patient may remain in the hospital, and the requirement that a patient be allowed to see specialists only if referred by an assigned doctor.

Various types of healthcare programs have been proposed. The universal healthcare program proposes healthcare coverage for all eligible residents of a region that often includes medical, dental, and mental healthcare. Most of the costs are met through a single-payer system (where payment of healthcare providers comes out of a single fund), or national health insurance. Universal healthcare has been implemented in all wealthy, industrialized countries with the exception of the United States. It is also provided in many developing countries and is the trend worldwide.

The common denominator in universal healthcare programs, according to Lyle Schofield in his article "Missing the Meaning of Health Care Reform," is some form of government action aimed at extending access to healthcare as widely as possible and setting minimum standards. Most countries implement universal healthcare through legislation, regulation, and taxation. Legislation and regulation dictate what care must be provided, to whom, and on what basis. The bulk of the cost comes from both compulsory insurance and tax revenue. In some countries universal healthcare entails government involvement including managing the system directly; however, many countries use a mixture of public and private healthcare.

The world's healthcare systems center on the treatment of symptoms, not the total healing of diseases according to the article, "Shifting America from Sick Care to Genuine Wellness." This article states, "The problem is we have systematically neglected wellness and disease prevention."

Economists have determined that the world economy is based on an aggregation of wealth and power. Political systems also stand in this vein. Together, economic and political agencies, such as the Food and Drug Administration (FDA) and the Federal Trade Commission (FTC), control the entire process of agriculture and legal drugs from what goes into food substances to the creation of pharmaceutical concoctions (Trudeau 25). These and other federal agencies form financial and political alliances that control the health of nations.

Controlling health means government entities can dictate

people's lifespan and destinies. It is important to note that those who create laws and policies regarding the growing, cultivating, creating, and distribution of food substances can also create systems that benefit their personal agendas. If a government agency dictates to medical establishments what medical procedures they can practice and what medicines they can dispense, then it is very likely they dominate the industries involved and regulate the choices of the citizens these policies ultimately affect.

For example, according to researcher Kevin Trudeau in his book, *Natural Cures*:

> Americans spend over $2 trillion a year on health care, yet American infant mortality is higher than twenty other developing countries. Americans consume over half of all the drugs manufactured in the world. There are over 200,000 nonprescription drugs on the market; there are over 30,000 prescription medications. Doctors write over 3 billion prescriptions each year. The average American has over thirty different prescription and nonprescription drugs in their medicine cabinets. The bottom line: The only winners in the cure and prevention of disease are the drug companies and the healthcare companies themselves (Trudeau 10).

Government agencies regulate the healthcare systems of most countries, including America and other countries in the Western world, according to *The New York Times* writer Kevin Sack. The same agencies that regulate food, water, and pharmaceutical drugs also regulate the policies around these industry giants and set procedures for them to follow (Trudeau 27). Furthermore, the same agencies that regulate large, publicly-traded companies usually hold stock in these companies (Trudeau 27).

This practice would seem to be a conflict of interests. It stands to reason that these industries are in business to make a profit for themselves and their shareholders. It is not uncommon for industry lobbyists to undergird a member of Congress (the legislative body responsible for creating laws in government) in order to pass laws that would be in the best interests of their clients (large businesses). It is quite common for lobbyists or interest groups to persuade members of Congress to vote for a piece of legislation that would benefit those they represent (Trudeau 24, 25). Lobbyists can also make large donations to a legislator's favorite charity or school in exchange for a favorable vote.

Even in civilized nations physicians are told what to propagate as "medicine" by associations regulated by federal food and drug agencies. A doctor cannot tell a patient to take three whole apples daily for the next seven days and call next week to see how the patient is feeling. Apples cannot be patented or trademarked; therefore they cannot be sold as medicinal. In other words, no one in the pharmaceutical industry (the industry that researches and creates legal drugs) can make a profit from an apple because no one in the drug industry created the apple.

Unquestionably, there are dilemmas that surround the healthcare industry especially when it is regulated by those that can be bought and sold at the expense of the health of the nation. According to the article, "The U.S. Health Care System," from the University of Maine, not all nations have this intermingled administration of healthcare, politics, and corporate business, but far too many follow this pursuit. It is the way of systematizing healthcare from the world's perspective for the profit of the powerful and the wealthy.

KINGDOM OF GOD CONSCIOUSNESS CONCERNING HEALTHCARE

In the Garden of Eden, before the fall or disobedient act of Adam, the first man, there was no sickness or disease on the earth. Once separation from God through sin resulted, Adam incurred all the malignancies of disobedience, including sickness, disease, and death (paraphrased Genesis 3:17-19).

Since the disobedient act of the first man and woman in the garden there has been the constant desire to return to perfect health, from searches for the fountain of youth to the latest miracle pill. Mankind is on a quest for perfect health outside of God's remedy given to counteract the effects of sins. God's answer to deterioration includes obeying His laws concerning every aspect of human life.

In the Kingdom of God, believers must understand that perfect health is only found in Christ's redeeming act of death on the cross. Now believers can "die to" or avoid the curses (pronouncements of evil) brought on by "one man's disobedience," and live in divine health because of "one man's grace." These declarations of punishment were consequences of disobedience to God as with Adam in his willful act of rebellion in the Garden of Eden. A curse is the affliction of the godless. The prophet Isaiah, in the Old Testament scriptures, exclaimed about the Lamb of God who would come. "Surely He has borne our griefs, and carried our sorrows; yet we esteemed Him stricken, smitten by God and afflicted... And by His stripes we are healed" (Isaiah 52:4a, 5b).

A Kingdom of God consciousness allows the believer to

live in the sphere where God dwells and where God's culture is the dominating factor. In the Creator there is no sickness or disease. Even if a believer subjects himself to the elements of the curse (the fallen state of mankind unreconciled to Christ's redemption; not submitted to the saving grace of Christ), there are ways that true healing (eradication of any ailment as Jesus in His earthly ministry healed people of all types of disease and sickness according to Matthew 4:23) could possibly take place by obeying natural laws of health through diet, exercise, and proper rest. Doctors or medicine can be avenues through which the body can achieve healing.

Physical healing can also miraculously manifest through God's ministers. Jesus explained in James 5:14-15: "Is anyone among you sick? Let him call for the elders of the church, and let them pray over him, anointing him with oil in the name of the Lord. And the prayer of faith will save the sick, and the Lord will raise him up." Healing also results through confession of faith. According to Mark 11:23: "For assuredly I say to you, whoever says to this mountain, be removed and be cast into the sea, and does not doubt in his heart, but believes those things that he says will be done, he will have whatever he says." When one believes in the Word of God, healing can occur and diseases and sicknesses can be eradicated from the body and soul.

Restoration from physical and emotional diseases can happen through obeying God's laws of forgiveness. Forgiveness is the release of a debt or wrong so that the offended would not carry the weight of the offense. Romans 14:21 explains: "It is good neither to eat meat nor drink wine nor do anything by which your brother stumbles or is offended or is made weak."

Contentment and the release of stress play an important role in nurturing healing and bringing wholeness in the body.

Every believer must spend the appropriate time sorting through and understanding how God's Kingdom works concerning health. Sickness and disease of body or soul are not God's intended will for mankind; therefore, through the atoning work of Christ, his death on the cross, healing became the inheritance of God's people. Isaiah 53:5 speaks of the atoning work of Christ where healing is concerned: "But He was wounded for our transgressions, He was bruised for out iniquities; the chastisement for our peace was upon Him, and by His stripes we are healed."

Through his death, Jesus brought unity between God and man. He also restored mankind to his original freedom from disease. Jesus came with the answer to sickness which believers can stand on, knowing that healing belongs to them as a gift from Christ; He suffered not for Himself but for mankind to restore man's relationship with God. God's aim is to renew and restore man's position as one who walks with the Creator in unbroken fellowship.

One walks in the fullness of God through a progressive, continual fellowship with God and His word. John 15:4-5 states: "Abide in Me, and I in you. As the branch cannot bear fruit of itself, unless it abides in the vine, neither can you, unless you abide in Me. I am the vine; you are the branches. He who abides in Me, and I in him, bears much fruit; for without Me you can do nothing." Continuing in the words and teachings of God denotes the title of "disciple" or one who follows the teachings of another; a learner or pupil (Strong 154). Abiding in and continually learning of God through His scriptural teachings engenders becoming like Christ, or abiding in His fullness.

WORLD'S SYSTEM OF EDUCATION

The system of education, according to *Webster's College Dictionary*, is "[an ordered and comprehensive] act or process of imparting or acquiring general knowledge and of developing the powers of reasoning and judgment." The education of children in societies began through the art of following by example and through oral traditions of storytelling. These skills were later developed into drawn pictures or codes that became written words transmitted to generations, preserving culture and societal ways of life. Education professor Gerald Gutek, in his article, "The History of Education," states: "Soon after written instructions became common, the extension of basic information developed into formal education as far back as 1770."

The educational system in the United States became compulsory (required) in 1852 in the state of Massachusetts through state statues and constitutional provisions (Gutek). State and federal governments administrate most of the public education in America including elementary, secondary, and higher-level education (universities and colleges). Government regulation of education has mandated that the atmosphere of learning cannot be limited based on the social or economic status of students or their families, nor can it be discriminatory based on ethnicity, religion, nationality, or physical handicaps.

For example, the Supreme Court ruling in 1954 concerning the segregation of public schools in America based on race set the tone for legally integrating the school systems for the first time in American history ("Brown v. Board of

Education"). This verdict sought to achieve racial balance in the schools and within the districts. This and prior cases established the presence of government intervention in public and private educational systems.

The word "system" according to *Webster's College Dictionary*, means "a coordinated body of methods or a scheme or plan of procedure; organizational scheme." When the word "system" is used regarding the world's educational methods, the word denotes a "scheme." There is a scheme in the world concerning the education and the infiltration of the minds of men. What an individual believes is what that person will do and become.

There is a push in the world's educational system to enthrone the human capacity and ingenuity of thoughts and knowledge. This system of methods go hand-in-hand with all the other systems previously mentioned. Whatever one ideologically thinks and pursues can be legitimized in the world of economics, politics, legality, and government. Controlling the mind of man is equivalent to controlling wealth, healthcare, legislation, and life.

Education is one way the world gains the power to control the thoughts of nations through controlling what is taught and how it is taught. The educational arena is infiltrated with ideas, thoughts, and mental exercises that have their roots in the deification of the intellect. Great scholars of old—Aristotle, Homer, Socrates, John Dewey, Isaac Newton—were very influential in how education is administrated in the world today. They still play a decisive role in the way men of all nations think. Viewpoints inherited from these and other scholars epitomize worshipping at the feet of novel ideas, from government social systems to laws of physics constructed by Sir

Isaac Newton, concerning the effects of motion when force is exerted (Fowler, Michael, "Isaac Newton").

The application of reason is the mainstay of the world's system of education in schools and universities, in business, and in government. It seems the world greatly desires to categorize and compartmentalize information and knowledge in order to boast of its understanding or familiarity with the strategy of learning. Man is obsessed with finding ways to explain his plight in order to make sense of it and feel he has some control. The educational system is a way in which man invokes his ideas and research to provide answers to the challenges of life. These renderings preclude having to find answers in some unknown entity outside man's physical senses. This is the world's way of attempting to control and order the world through intellect outside of unexplainable reasoning. This mentality is where secular humanism begins.

Secular humanism—philosophical understanding "through critical reason, factual evidence, and scientific methods, rather than by faith or mysticism—is using the thoughts, ideas, and experiences of mankind to erect a social world of right and wrong, good and bad" (Charles 90). Morality, according to this way of thinking, is based on subjective opinions garnered through reason, logic, and the superiority of ideas. The ancient Greek philosophers exalted the knowledge of men to construct their own way in the world, thus, "they lived within their own opinion" (Charles 93).

Even the present-day educational system, derived from ancient Greek humanism (Charles 92), has taken on the role of the teacher of ideology to inculcate humanistic doctrine. It puts the citizenry in a dependent mode of going to college, attaining a degree of learning, finding a job in some industry, paying taxes, and keeping the society supplied with wage-earners to support the government's agenda—good or bad. "The whole purpose of Greek education was to subordinate the individual to the needs of the state" (Charles 93). "Studies indicate that 75% of American college professors teach that there is no such thing as right and wrong. Instead they treat questions of good and evil as relative to individual values and cultural diversity" (Charles 95).

This process of evaluating morality in universities has given way to the phenomenon of situational ethics. Situational ethics promote non-compliance with moral absolutes. This school of thought relegates right and wrong to contextual evidence. Situational ethics embrace a code in which meeting the needs of each situation is what determines right and wrong. The educational system of most developing nations indoctrinates and keeps the focus on needs, concerns, and self-aggrandizement of the individual.

KINGDOM OF GOD CONSCIOUSNESS OF EDUCATION

Secular humanism must be replaced with God's truth. Education outside of God and His way of rulership is unwise. According to 1 Corinthians 8:1: "Knowledge puffs up [makes arrogant], but love edifies [builds up]."

In the Kingdom of God education serves as a tool by which God's pre-destined plan is perpetuated in the hearts and minds of mankind. Knowledge of God is having consciousness of God; His Word and His methods. This is the new paradigm of learning in the Kingdom of God where there is increased awareness, acknowledgement, and cognizance of God as Teacher and Revealer of Truth (Charles 105). There has to be a pursuit of God's holy wisdom, not the wisdom of the world which is sensual, earthly, and unprofitable. The first century church in Corinth was instructed by the Apostle Paul: "For

Knowledge of God is having consciousness of God; His Word and His methods.

the wisdom of this world is foolishness with God" (1 Corinthians 3:19).

The consciousness of the believer must push past the temptation to rest on the comforts of mankind's greatest false mantra: that he is his own god. Anytime an individual operates outside God's culture and methods he operates in his own strength, relying on the limitations of human capabilities and empty ingenuity. The Godless man is a dangerous man, and a man in danger.

The educational system of God's Kingdom centers on the truth that God desires to infiltrate the believer with true knowledge and support that knowledge with Godly wisdom, insight, and understanding for a well-rounded believer operating on earth in the capacity of God's ambassador.

In the Hebrew scriptural text, the educational system of God includes God instructing parents to recite His laws to their children: "You shall teach them [Laws of Moses] diligently to your children" (Deuteronomy 6:7). In the culture of the Israelite community it was the father's responsibility to tell his children about the miraculous events of the nation, including

Anytime an individual operates outside God's culture and methods he operates in his own strength, relying on the limitations of human capabilities and empty ingenuity. The Godless man is a dangerous man, and a man in danger.

the Exodus out of Egyptian slavery (Exodus 10:2; 13:8). It was the duty of the Levites (members of the Hebrew tribe of Levi) to provide instruction in both religious ritual and practical application to the people: "They shall teach your laws to Jacob, and your instruction to Israel" (Deuteronomy 33:10). After the Babylonian exile, Ezra—priestly scribe leading 5,000 captured Israelites of Babylon back to their home city of Jerusalem in 459 BC—gathered the people together and read and expounded the Torah before them (Nehemiah 8:2-3; 8). "It was Ezra (who read the Book of the Law of Moses) who instituted the Bible reading every Monday and Thursday morning on the days when people came to the local markets" ("Judaism." Just the Facts on Religion).

In the early Israelite religious culture, boys as young as five years of age were instructed in the study of the Bible and at thirteen years old were obligated to keep the Commandments. Summed up in the writings of author Strack Hermann, in his work, *Introduction to the Talmud and Midrash:*

> The Jewish law required that the parents begin the child's religious education at the earliest possible age, and declares that as soon as a child begins to speak, he must be taught the verse, 'Moses charged us with the Teaching as the heritage of the congregation of Jacob' (Deuteronomy 33:4).

In God's system of education after one has confessed Jesus Christ as Lord and Savior his spiritual education commences, and it is available to all who have an ability to learn and understand the biblical tenants of God. For example, Jesus instructed the people in Matthew 11:29: "Take my yoke upon you and learn from Me, for I am gentle and lowly in heart, and you will find rest for your souls."

In the Kingdom of God educational system one is instructed "not [to] be conformed to this world but be transformed by the renewing of your mind" (Romans 12:2). The word "conformed" means "accommodating oneself to a model or pattern; to fashion like" (Strong 244). The people were instructed to forego being like the age or the system in which they lived which was ungodly. It was the believer's responsibility to renew or refocus their own minds to conformity with the ideals of the Kingdom of God. This transformed and renewed mind would come as one submitted to the understanding and practice of God's will. Agreement with this world's systems and ways of living would prove detrimental to the believer's life.

In God's paradigm of learning, the believer must study God's Word to understand Him and the teachings of Christ

for proper spiritual development. In 2 Timothy 3:16, the Apostle Paul encourages the young pastor during the difficult times: "All scripture is given by inspiration of God, and is profitable for doctrine, for reproof, for correction, for instruction in righteousness." The scriptures are understood as a guide of the believer's life and a road map for his spiritual and personal journey. Therefore, the biblical text must be taught and studied in order that the application of God's truth can be employed. 2 Timothy 2:15 makes this demand: "Study to shew thyself approved unto God, a workman that needeth not to be ashamed, rightly dividing the word of truth" (King James Version). Studying involves giving oneself over earnestly to a task and exerting oneself with diligence (Strong 232). Diligent study of the Word of truth is the pivotal key to the educational system of God. Without study there is no informed knowledge of God's character, His nature, or His will in the believer's life. Consequently, righteous instructions are difficult to apply without fundamental instructions and personal application of God's Word.

WORLD'S SYSTEM OF RELIGION

Religion, at its core, is mankind's attempt to explain, reach, and interpret God; it is subjective systematized views of God (Musser and Price, *A New Handbook of Christian Theology* 397). Because mankind possesses a spiritual nature he has an innate desire to worship and relate to the spirit realm. God gave mankind a spirit when He instructed the God-Head (Christ and the Holy Spirit) to create Adam. God said: "Let Us make man in Our image, according to Our likeness" (Genesis 1:26).

"God is a spirit," according to the Apostle John's recording

(John 4:24). God does not exist in bodily form, although He has the power to manifest in a body. God is spiritual reality and His nature is spirit. God is supernatural essence; an incorporeal being. God created man like Himself, with a spirit.

This spiritual nature of man was created by God and came from God. It then is very natural for mankind to desire

Because mankind possesses a spiritual nature he has an innate desire to worship and relate to the spirit realm

relationship with his creator and to establish institutions that accommodate this longing. However, when religious institutions are intertwined with politics, economics, militant aggression, and the desire to control, conquer, and dominate, many problems erupt.

Religion has been the starting point of most every evil political fantasy of mankind—from political cults, nationalists, and totalitarian dictators to anarchist groups touting their "rights" and not their "responsibilities" (Harrison 200).

There have been many times in the history of man that a religious iconic government evolved into the national identity of a country. For instance, Islamic aggression against the Western world bases its military thrusts on the holy war, the jihad. Pierre Tristam, in his article "Jihad: Middle East Issues," explains: "Jihad in Arabic is a noun meaning 'struggle.' The Sunni scholars refer to Jihad as the sixth pillar of Islam and it is considered the religious duty of Muslims." Although politically and militantly infused, this regime is thoroughly based in the national religious sentiments of Islam. In the article "Jihad" in *Wikipedia, the Free Encyclopedia*, the nature of Jihad is summed up in this account:

Jihad requires Muslims to struggle in the way of God, or to struggle to improve one's self and society. There are four major categories of Jihad:

> Jihad against one's self; Jihad of the tongue; Jihad of the hand; and Jihad of the sword. Islamic military focuses on relegating the practice of Jihad of the sword, the only form of warfare permissible under Islamic law, and, thus the term Jihad is usually used in manuals in reference to military combat.

In tandem, the Roman Catholic Church, being the largest Christian community, is religiously joined to its economic and political power in the world representing one-sixth of the world's population. According to Orthodox Bishop and author Timothy Ware:

> The Roman Catholic Church is a communion of the Western Rite and the Eastern Catholic Churches. The Catholic Church's doctrines rest on hierarchical structure of the Church, Apostolic Succession, the episcopate, and the priesthood. The Catholic tradition's highest earthly authority in matters of faith, morality and governance is the Pope. The Pope is considered Sovereign of the Vatican City State, who holds supreme authority in concert with the College of Bishops (Successors of the Apostles), of which the Pope is head (Ware 239).

The Catholic Church defines its mission as spreading the

gospel of Jesus Christ, administering the sacraments, and exercising charity. It operates social institutions throughout the world including schools, universities, hospitals, missions, and shelters.

> Through apostolic succession (succession of bishops through an uninterrupted line traceable back to the original twelve Apostles of Jesus), the Church believes itself to be the continuation of the Christian community founded by Jesus in the consecration of Saint Peter. The Church also believes that it is guided by the Holy Spirit of God, and so protected from falling into doctrinal error (Ware 248).

This religious center takes its position at the helm of world politics and imposes its religious beliefs on the socio-political culture of nations because of its sovereignty as a governmental entity (Musser and Price, eds, 504-508). Musser and Price also examine the Vatican city-state:

> The Vatican in Rome is the seat of the Catholic world. It is a sovereign city-state, an ecclesiastical monarchy, ruled by the Bishop of Rome—the Pope. The Pope's position as a life-long monarch has full power as the legislative, executive, and judicial executor of this country. This religious ruler resides in the Apostolic Palace of the Vatican. Vatican City has its own military, police, bank, and the only automatic teller machine (ATM) with instructions in Latin.

It is clear to see the juxtapositioning of government and political agencies with national religious identity of this nation.

A state religion is a universal religion of a nation. "A state religion (official religion or state church) is a religious body or creed (statement of belief) officially endorsed by the state" (Gaustad 33). State religions are examples of the official or government-sanctioned establishment of religion. "The Armenian Orthodox Church established in 301 A.D., was the first national church" (Kjeilen, "Armenian Orthodox Church").

There are countries that recognize official religions as their state religions. Roman Catholicism has been adopted as the civil religion of regions such as Monaco and Vatican City. Afghanistan and Egypt as well as Iran and Pakistan have declared Islam as their national religion. The United States, a secular jurisdiction, does not recognize any civil religion.

An example of world religion is that of Judaism. Judaism is tied to national and ethnic tenants. According to the article "What is Judaism?" by Tracey Rich, Judaism is the culture, religion, social practices, and beliefs of Jews. The religion of the Jews is characterized by monotheism (belief in one god), a belief in a divine covenant making them God's chosen people, and ethnic and territorial identity (the 'Promised Land' especially the land of Canaan which is present-day Jerusalem), special laws and ritual practices, and Messianism (belief that a Messiah will establish the Jews as the ruling nation and conquer all enemies). The laws of the Jews trace their historical context back to Moses (Israel's leader who freed them from Egyptian slavery) and Mosaic Law (the Pentateuch, the first five books of the Bible) (paraphrased Exodus 19 and 20).

Political Judaism is closely associated with King David who set up his capital in Judah and planned the construction of the temple which his son Solomon carried out (paraphrased 1

Kings 1:30, 1 Kings 6). During Babylonian captivity (586-538 B.C.), Judaism was consolidated and the Mosaic Law was written (Rich, "What is Judaism?"). As befits a theocracy (belief in one-god rulership), the distinction between divine law and civil law is blurred. All Jews subscribed to the fact that God was supreme power and His commands were established as the law and there was no distinction between the civil law of God and the religious law of God. The Mosaic Law (torah) was the most sacred writing in Judaism and was completed around the fifth century B.C. It was interpreted by the Talmud (which includes religious and civil laws not in the Torah proper) and gives explanation of them. "The Midrash (includes tradition law and minor precepts) keeps close to scripture and it covers a period of approximately ten centuries (Hermann 11-12).

The high priest served as head of state and administered both religious and civil law. Rabbis, religious teachers usually ordained by the Sanhedrin Council of Jewish judges, were both interpreters of the law and civil judges of penal cases. The text of the law was "fixed" or correctly written by hand by scribes. They recorded interpretations of the law as they occurred through time. Scribes not only meticulously wrote the law, but they also served as dictators of historical records for kings and royalty. Pharisees were a sect that dedicated themselves to the exact practice of oral and written laws. They were a political party—eclectic, popular, and democratic—that spoke against the economic and cultural forces of first-century Jews. They were part of the divided sects of Jews during the first century.

When the Romans destroyed the Jewish temple in 70 A.D. and occupied the country, as a nation, Jews were dispersed and fragmented. Their extreme religious interpretation went from fundamentalism to a mixture of rabbinical customs and philosophical thought. The Jewish Diaspora expanded from Eastern Europe both west and east. In the early twentieth century Jews were persecuted and lived in Nazi ghettos. Discrimination against them (anti-Semitism) in Germany became wide-spread and prominent after erroneous accusations of spying against the German military.

After the Second World War and the Nazi-conspired genocide of millions, surviving Jews advocated for the reestablishment of a Jewish homeland. The longed-for nation was established in Palestine in 1948. Although they returned to a portion of their homeland, it was not theocratic. It was secular and divided.

KINGDOM OF GOD SYSTEM OF RELATIONSHIP

In the Gospel according to Matthew 15:6b Jesus warned the scribes and Pharisees: "You make God's law to mean nothing so you can keep your own laws [religious traditions]" (Worldwide English New Testament Version). The religions and traditions of men that facilitate their personal agendas do not qualify them for God's favor. In contrast, Jesus designated men as "hypocrites" who used religious rituals in the place of heartfelt sincerity toward God that comes only through personal relationship with Him governed by obedience and submission to His laws. Therefore, in the Kingdom of God, religion does not exist. Religion is man's attempt to reach the eternal God by his own cunning and ingenuity. Religion is man's way of explaining God within the limitations of his personal ambitions and agendas.

In the Kingdom of God, religion does not exist. Religion is man's attempt to reach the eternal God by his own cunning and ingenuity. Religion is man's way of explaining God within the limitations of his personal ambitions and agendas.

With a Kingdom of God consciousness, one must conclude that God is primarily concerned with relationship, not religion. The Apostle Paul wrote in Galatians 3:26: "For you are all sons of God through faith in Christ Jesus" (NKJV). God therefore intended to have a family of believers through Jesus. Jesus Himself referred to God as "Father," (John 14:9b) indicating the type of association and involvement God desires to have with His believers: "He who has seen Me has seen the Father."

Relationship is God's agenda and creation, not man's. Relationship is what God says about Himself; religion is how man interprets what God said. Religion is the product of mankind inventing his own righteousness or right standing with the God of Heaven. A right relationship with the eternal Father prompts one to seek God on God's terms. One cannot earn, work for, or attain right standing with God in his own strength. The Apostle Paul communicated with the Roman church in 56 A.D. saying:

For I bear them witness that they have a zeal for God but not according to knowledge. For they being ignorant of God's righteousness, and seeking to establish their own righteousness, have not submitted to the righteousness of God. For Christ is the end of the law for righteousness to everyone who believes (Romans 10:2-4, NKJV).

God's righteousness exists outside man's structures and abilities to maneuver through his ideological religious concepts. God sets the parameters of the divine system of righteousness for mankind's return to a consciousness of God.

According to the above scriptural text, Christ is the way back to God and all that Christ did has to be acknowledged and accepted into one's own life. Accepting this divine truth is the recognition of corruptible man's right relationship with God through Jesus Christ, not by constructing mental perusals. God's system of religion starts with the intention of man to live in right relationship with God and the methodology of God achieves this right standing through acceptance of Jesus Christ as the fulfillment of the requirements and demands of the law.

Consequently, the Kingdom of God is not about a system of religion, but a system of relationship with God through His Son. The evil in the heart of humanity may propagate a philosophical ideology shrouded in a religious context. But the goodness of the Holy Deity propagates unbroken fellowship with the Creator through belief in His divine strategy of the gift of righteousness.

Chapter

TRADITIONAL CHURCH CONSCIOUSNESS

The traditional church has made better strides into finding a stance in Kingdom of God consciousness than have the world systems. However, the modern, twenty-first century church has vastly departed from the Apostles' teachings and doctrines through religious traditions, secularization, and institutionalization of the church.

Secularity is views and beliefs with no Godly affiliation. Secularization rejects all forms of faith and worship and promotes the importance of human reason separate from God. Institutionalization is the social construct that formulates acceptable patterns of behavior fundamental to the establishment.

Secularization holds the worldview that faith (belief in God) and the public realm should be kept apart, and that faith has no place in public life: hence the ideology of separation of Church and State. This separation of civic and church interests is legally instituted in the United States. It is a dichotomy of the sacred and the worldly. Secularization draws its intellectual roots from Greek and Roman philosophies of human autonomy and reason. Institutionalization has the capacity to undergird secularization in its ability to erect a systemic model of social control. Institutionalization hinges on the hierarchical structure of "power over" and lies outside critical judgment and reflective change. Institutionalization places the social construct in a state of unchanging monotony.

To institutionalize or secularize the church is to constrict the movement of God. If not nourished daily the church in its secularized or institutionalized form loses its power and then becomes a structure within a world dictated by human wisdom and reason. The power of the church and its believers is antipathy to secularization and institutionalization. The traditional church has now supplanted the original revelation of the church given through God's Apostles.

TRADITIONS

The first-century church experienced a flood of new believers. The new Christians (those who followed the teachings of Christ) represented every level of socio-economic, ethnic, and philosophical background. Therefore, it was an imperative project to document the fundamental teachings of the church. The Apostles' teachings and church traditions enveloped God's redemptive plan of grace for the church. Author J.N.D Kelly, in his book, *Early Christian Doctrines*, points out: "Because there was such a radical departure or extension of Hebraic theology, the first-century church struggled to comply with this divine paradigm shift" (Kelly

189). Therefore, many teachers and apostles spent their lives teaching, instructing, and rendering revelation to the infant church regarding this new epoch in religious history.

The spread of this new gospel, or good news, expanded from Jerusalem (Palestine) throughout the Mediterranean west. Although Christianity started out with mostly Jewish followers, it soon blossomed to include all races, ethnicities, languages, and cultures with various social, political, and religious backgrounds. They all sought to live out the revelatory mandate of Jesus Christ, the risen Son of God. First-century Christians, made up of Jews and many others, recognized that the messianic promise of the Old Testament scriptures had been culminated in Christ. The bond of Judaism and Christianity was solidified, giving Christianity a legitimate origin of impetus.

The Apostle Peter (one of the original disciples of Jesus Christ) and the Apostle Paul were predominant figures in the first-century church. Peter mostly instructed Jewish converts whereas Paul, after frustrating attempts to encourage Jewish believers, proceeded to devote himself totally to Gentiles in teaching and apostolic service (paraphrased Acts 28:28). The Apostles taught believers that the Law of Moses and the Prophets were fulfilled through the sacrifice Jesus made on the cross when He was crucified yet without sin. They conveyed that this atoning sacrifice was what bought mankind's salvation and unbroken fellowship with God the Father.

These church pioneers upheld the teachings of Jesus as well as instituted church policy and structure through the spiritual traditions of the church—the Eucharist (Communion), baptism which is water immersion typifying admission of the recipient into Christian faith, faith (reliance of total personality on God through Jesus Christ), triune being of God (God the Father, Son and Holy Spirit), Jesus born fully deity and fully human, virgin birth (impregnation of a virgin to conceive the Messiah), the role of bishops and other church leaders, grace (unmerited gift of divine favor); justification (to be made righteous; right relationship with God, and all the fundamentals of the faith (Chadwick 16, 32).

The spiritual traditions of the church came by revelatory instruction from the Spirit of Christ through these men of faith as well as their experienced leadership. Because the first-century church was in its infancy and because of the various socio-cultural backgrounds of its members, organization and administration had to be established. However, expounding upon the texts of the Hebrew scriptures was equally as important in order to bring new believers into the church's revolutionary movement.

Paul, arguably the most prominent figure in first-century Christendom, established churches throughout Asia, Africa, and Europe from 46-62 A.D. The church expanded from Jerusalem all the way north to Rome. Even during times of great persecution and "official suspicion" by imperial and religious councils, Paul continued to make great strides in proselytizing the regions ignorant of the truth of Christ (Chadwick 16, 21). He taught the fundamental elements of the faith, giving great dialogues on church governance and personal responsibility. The Apostle persisted in the focus on living up to the charge of Christ's transforming work in the souls of men. Paul was dedicated to his faith and never lost passion for his mission:

> Paul was totally committed to his call to spread the gospel and establish churches throughout the known world. He lived what he wrote, that the gifts and the calling of God are irrevocable. His life demonstrated three basic concepts of his leadership: 1) He was committed to the goals and spirit of his call; 2) He translated his objectives to the lives of his followers and bore with all necessary hardship in pursuing that end; 3) He was alert to change. He adapted to cultural, social, and political changes and thus never lost his relevancy (Hayford 1676).

MODERN CHURCH TRADITIONS

The church continued to spread the gospel to every part of the society of men from the infant first-century thrusts to the missionary advances of the fifteenth through the nineteenth centuries and beyond. The church has made an indelible mark on world communities throughout the centuries. Globally, it has impacted the world and set the tone for acceptance of the transformative work of

Traditions, with their false sense of superiority, stagnate the future by holding tightly to the past

Christ. However, in the twenty-first century, it has been noted that the church in this time has deviated from the fundamental Christian faith of the apostles and teachings of

Christ to a more easily-tolerated level of comfortable existence.

There has been a slow movement away from the spiritual traditions of the ancient church and its formative work. The notion of the church as a social platform has emerged and has even sanctioned hypocrisy (pretense or false profession of virtues), institutional slavery (systematizing of humans as property), and denominationalism (divided religious groups). The modern church seems to be divided over race, socio-economic class, forms of worship, and general theology. The consciousness of the modern church focuses on organization overshadowing service.

Modern-day traditions of the church as a whole huddle around the personal lives and agendas of individuals rather than on the mandate of God: "To make disciples of all the nations, baptizing them in the name of the Father, Son, and the Holy Spirit" (Matthew 28:19). The traditions of the church, especially in the West, generally focus on the economic strength of individual churches, the prominence of gifted individuals within the church, and the power of denominational categories. These church traditions distract from God's original mandate to make disciples.

Church traditions are among the greatest enemies to the viable true church of God. In Jesus' thrust to teach the scribes and Pharisees, He pointed out to them: "Thus, you have made the commandments of God of no effect by your tradition" (Matthew 15:66). Traditions, with their false sense of superiority, stagnate the future by holding tightly to the past. It is not tradition that the church must adhere to; it is fundamental truths as proclaimed by scriptural texts given to the Apostles and Prophets of God. The character and nature of God never change; He is by essence "unchangeable" (Malachi 3:6). However, God's methodology does give way to new dispensations and new movements. For example, God moved from the age of Davidic temples to the age of the Church; from the Law of Moses to Jesus Christ, the fulfillment of the law (paraphrased Matthew 5:17).

Traditions are experiences one has journeying through time. Therefore, traditions in and of themselves are not inappropriate. However, traditions can be what God said about yesterday and not what God says today. In this sense, tradition can pose as an enemy to God's "proceeding Word" (paraphrased Matthew 4:4). It is easy for a believer to stop where God has been. But the true test of church relevance is to be at the place where God is currently. Anything other than this position of obedience to God makes the church impotent and unequipped to handle its God-given responsibilities on the earth. As strongly protested by Bishop Eddie L. Long in his work, *Taking Over*: "What I am tired of is this man-made, man-dominated, man-centered façade that is posing as the true church" (Long 31).

SECULARIZATION

What happened to the life-changing force of the first-century church that "turned cities upside down" with charismatic fervor for a loving God? How has the church not been able to maintain its potent surge of theological influence in today's world? What happened to the move of the church to equip, change, and galvanize strength for the sake of Divine will?

The definition of secularization is the act of separating the sacred from the worldly; freedom from the rules and teachings of one's faith. Secularization involves the activity of removing the influence of God and placing importance on the reasoning power of man through facts and evidence. It is the deification of human intellect and autonomy from the supernatural, especially within the church.

Secularization has made constant inroads into the church and stripped from it the power given by the omnipotent God.

Through the rise of the preeminence of empirical science and rationality, the influence of the church has gradually lessened.

Many through the Age of Enlightenment focused on knowledge and facts rather than faith (believing what is unseen). The Enlightenment was an intellectual movement in Europe (Age of Reason) that focused on facts, reason, and intellect rather than faith in God. It was the celebration of human reasoning and ingenuity. Within this movement was the commitment to the scientific method and factual evidence in an attempt to resolve human dilemmas.

The Enlightenment was an intellectual and philosophical movement that put the focus on the mental supremacy of mankind. In European societies human reason became the source of authority. Philosophical rationality took the place of the influence of religion in government, academics, and the economic and social arenas. The foundation of ethical and moral principles relied on the application of reason, personal experience, and science. The indoctrination of the Age of Enlightenment systematically engendered a philosophy that exalted man's earthly wisdom above the supernatural wisdom of God. Furthermore, this movement found its way into the church.

SECULARIZED CHURCH

With the invasion of secular traditions intertwined with spiritual traditions, the church in the modern day is losing the battle for God's Kingdom order with a consciousness of the world. Living, thinking, and behaving apart from the directives of God's divine instruction places the believer on the outside of the biblical text. When there is friendship with the world, in the sense that the world's order supplants God's order, then treason occurs in the courtroom of Heaven. There should be no mixture of the secular and the Kingdom of God's rulership.

In the Christian church today there is ecclesiastical permission to sanction same sex marriage, homosexuality, and other lifestyles directly opposing to God's precepts (paraphrased Leviticus 18:22; 20:13 and Romans 1:24-27). The world's perspective boasts that lifestyle is a personal choice, thus it should be acceptable even to church and religious structures. Unfortunately, religious structures as a whole challenge nothing. According to Bishop Eddie Long, Senior Pastor of New Birth Missionary Baptist Church:

> We have watered down the gospel to make it seeker-friendly. In doing so we have come into agreement with homosexuality, abortion, and countless other vital issues about which God's Word is clear; yet we choose to remain silent and do nothing. In God's eyes we are guilty of aiding and abetting when we remain silent while God says to speak! Everybody has an opinion, but nobody has a standard (Long 23, 44).

The church arena has also been used by ambitious politicians to engender voter support on policies and legislation not within the biblical framework of justice, fairness, love of God, neighbor, and self. Ecclesiastical bodies have relaxed the charge of Christ to preach, teach, and make Disciples of Christ, not of the world's systemic ideologies and separation from the true God. Politics should not influence the church; the church should influence and change national policies.

Another way secularization has found its way into the church world is through compromise with worldly practices and acceptance of persistent rebellion against God's Word. The Word of God expressly states: "There is now therefore no condemnation to those who are in Christ Jesus" (Romans 8:1).

This means there is no judgment, no reproof, and no blame for sins for those who stand in the position of Christ—accepting His work of reconciliation of mankind to God through His death on the cross. No judgment will be imputed to the believer who stands in his position of forgiveness by God through Christ. This is a positional truth bestowed on the believer who has taken the substitutional work of Christ as his own. However, once a believer stands outside his inherited right from a non-condemning God then all he does wrong will have consequences following—whatever is sown is what will be reaped (paraphrased Galatians 6:7).

When one accepts the atoning sacrifice of Christ and is placed in a state free of condemnation there is simultaneously no conformity to this world, to its thinking, behaving, and doing. Conforming to this present age is actually antithetical to the propagation of the truth of God. Conforming to the way of life of the world's systems positions one to be a "friend" of this world with a conscious mindset of the propaganda of this world's views. God explains that the believer should not allow this world's views to change his consciousness about God or to destroy his awareness of God.

Kingdom of God consciousness, apart from conformity to the secularization of the church world, presents a standard that demonstrates God's way to freedom from the bondage of human rationalism and intellectualism. Human rationalism is the school of thought that places credence on reason as the absolute authority for arriving at basic truth. Rationalism puts great emphasis on the mind's ability to discern coherence to the world. In rationalism, knowledge is derived from reason. Intellectualism is the attitude of devotion to the intellect. In this view, there is an emphasis on thinking with the absence of emotions. The two schools of thought are closely tied; however, the difference is seen in rationalism as knowledge and reason are the discerning of right and wrong whereas in Intellectualism it is the human will that ultimately decides the morality and ethical boundaries of actions.

Secular thought is in captivity to its own limitations, and therefore is in need of being rescued. The rescuing of the secular mindset comes through the power of life lived in the freedom of an all-sufficient God who liberates the captive soul.

This freedom has the ability to transform an unbeliever through the uncompromised lifestyle of a believer in Christ Jesus. This is the witness of Kingdom of God consciousness of a follower of God displayed alongside a secular world estranged from God.

Institutionalization of the Church

Institutions are human-made constructs confined by ideological concepts of tradition and culture. They are social arrangements that direct behavior in different ways. "An institution is a pattern of organization, behavior, relationships, laws or customs, and a long-established set of practices" (*Webster's College Dictionary*). Institutions provide structure and order to a program or foundation for its fundamental purposes. Institutions are usually systemic in nature, meaning once established, they take on a life of their own. Institutions are often inefficient and unresponsive to sudden changes in society due to demographic shifts, global interdependence, and technology.

Institutions serve to manage and direct individual, as well as organizational, behavior. Institutions have social purpose and permanence that order the lives and choices of people, thus channeling behavior. In other words, institutions have the capacity to control the lives and actions of people. The detriments of an institutionalized church start with the inherent liability of the construct of the institution itself. As aforementioned, an institution, once started, begins to take on a life of its own. Authors Stanley Eitzen and Maxine Baca-Zinn explain in their book, *In Conflict and Order:* "Institutions may be intentionally and deliberately created by people; however, institutions arise, develop and function in a pattern of social self-organization, which goes beyond the conscious intentions of the individual humans involved" (Eitzen and Baca-Zinn 47-49).

The institutionalized church continues in the stream of status quo passivity and docile religion (man-created construct used to interpret God). There is no power to initiate change for the community. A rigid institutional church can develop a consciousness that escapes present world realities settling for a preoccupation with the second coming of Christ. This is the mindset of an unwillingness to connect meaningfully with the world so as to deny responsibility to help change the world. The primary focus is on living in heaven away from the "unchangeable," ungodly world of this present time. The quest for the fulfillment of divine mandate for believers to "make disciples of the nations" may have been supplanted with the age of religious resignation. There is no quest to engage the world with transformative power from God's Spirit. The focus of the institutional church is on heaven where all the burdens can be laid down, or an overarching preoccupation with church organization and administration.

This escapism mentality renders the believer powerless and unaware of his covenant rights secured by God through Christ.

The salvation plan of God includes total restoration in every aspect of human life and endeavor. To have this consciousness through Kingdom of God mentality is the one force that rescues the escapist mentality of the institutionalized church.

"Form with no power" describes a church lost within structures, organizations, and institutions that conform to a personal agenda regardless of service to God. In his letter to the Roman church in 56 A.D., the Apostle Paul counsels Christians (followers of Christ) in the region: "Do not be conformed to this world, but be transformed by the renewing of your mind, that you may prove what is that good and acceptable and perfect will of God" (Romans 12:2). The word "world" in this passage literally means "age," referring to a godless system (Hayford 1707). Paul cautions believers in Rome to be careful not to accept the pattern of thinking induced by a worldly system. Roman Christians were expected to be devoted to the principles of the Kingdom of God in their daily lives.

There is an invisible and visible war waged for the souls of men by continually forcing conformity to this world's fruitless ways of thinking, being, and doing. This process perpetuates the cycle of disarming and captivating believers, leaving them unable to gain victory or enforce divine power. Similarly, Kenneth E. Hagin, author and teacher of the Bible for almost 70 years, pointed out to believers in his book, *The Believer's Authority*: "Our job is to enforce [Christ's] victory. His victory belongs to us, but we are to carry it out" (Hagin 29). Acts 1:8 speaks to the delegated power Christ gave to believers: "But you shall receive power when the Holy Spirit has come upon you..." In a similar manner, Jesus exclaimed in Luke 10:19: "Behold I give you authority to trample on serpents and scorpions, and over all the power of the enemy, and nothing shall by any means hurt you."

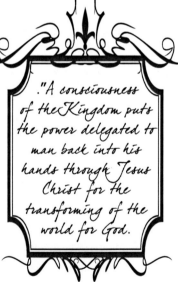

."A consciousness of the Kingdom puts the power delegated to man back into his hands through Jesus Christ for the transforming of the world for God.

Also, in the book of Matthew, Jesus is recorded as having called His twelve disciples, conferring power upon them: "He gave them power over unclean spirits, to cast them out, and to heal all kinds of sickness and all kinds of disease." A consciousness of the Kingdom puts the power delegated to man back into his hands through Jesus Christ for the transforming of the world for God.

There are no longer any moments to spare by involvement with passé religious formalities and unpurposeful church

activities. This is the pivotal moment to grasp the depth of God's divine intentions for victory in life on the earth. By now, the institutionalized church should be a relic of the past. The true church can no longer misrepresent the Kingdom of God.

There can no longer be loyalty to the creeds and constitutions of men without the inspiration of the Holy Scripture. The true church cannot institutionalize God and relegate the Creator to the limitations of man-made traditions and powerless church formulas.

This is the time for believers everywhere to take solace in the indemnification of the spiritual inheritance of Christ. Empty traditions, secularization, and the institutionalization of the church are no longer acceptable for those commissioned by God. This is the opportune moment for believers to engage the consciousness of the Kingdom of God so that there is a knowing, a pursuit of God, and not a pursuit of the next philosophy, church service, or great idea. This pursuit has the greatest ability to manifest where there is a consciousness of God; an awareness of God's being and doing, His culture, His methodology, His plan, and His agenda.

It is about time the body of believers focused on what God, through Jesus Christ, focused on throughout His earthly ministry. Bold steps need to be taken to reposition the church from where it is to where it needs to be as the voice and vessel of God on earth.

These steps will include radical, fundamental changes within the mind of every believer and a push toward a new God-conscious paradigm. The focus has to change from what is done on the outside in the form of religious ceremonies to what has manifested on the inside necessitating a revolutionary upheaval of the current religious mindset. There will be revival, but it will happen on the inside of every believer affecting change on the outside world.

The Kingdom of God has already commenced in the world. The challenge for most believers is to join the movement of God in creation. The changing of the guards has already transpired and the church is now facing a quickly-changing world. How the world will change is based on how believers willingly flow with the movement of the Kingdom of God.

> *There will be revival, but it will happen on the inside of every believer affecting change on the outside world.*

Dr. Karen M. Smith

SECTION 2

Chapter

5

KINGDOM OF GOD CONSCIOUSNESS

WHAT IS KINGDOM OF GOD CONSCIOUSNESS?

In the dimension of the Kingdom of God, true life and essence have been revealed, and true power has been fully clad. It is the dimension where one's being is the catalyst of change and transformation. It is a God-conscious atmosphere where miracles, signs, and wonders happen just because one appeared who operates in Kingdom dimensionality. In this dimension there is little effort and great peace. True identity is known, not only to the person in consideration, but to all existence in both heaven and earth. This is the dimension of true sonship unveiled and released on the earth. This is the Kingly and the Priestly anointing joining together for God's purposes and plans.

In the early Hebrew culture, after the rise of the kings, the king's consecration was for victory and the acquisition of the enemy's territory and property. In the Kingdom of God, this anointing is the empowerment for authority in the earth. Kingly entitlement is for believers' victory on the earth as they disperse Kingdom of God rulership. The role of the priest was to intercede for the people as he presented their requests and offerings to God. They were empowered to perform their role as intercessors. The anointing or the empowerment for the priests strengthened them as they prayed, interceded, and worshipped God in service to His people. This, in essence, is the full maturity of the believer who is not only a true son, but one who simultaneously establishes, transforms, subdues, and takes dominion.

The Kingdom of God is within one's heart, but this Kingdom has to be revealed to the soul who carries it. This inevitably is the position of the Holy Spirit, the revealer of all truth. The Kingdom within the believer is a Kingdom put into action by knowing and believing that it exists. Kingdom of God consciousness has a two-fold meaning. Firstly, it is a state or condition of awakening of the consciousness to a realization that this Kingdom truly exists and it maintains itself in the spirit and heart of the believer. Secondly, Kingdom of God consciousness is an awakening to the true identity and purpose of the believer who embraces it.

The Apostle Paul recognized that there is a three-dimensional aspect to man's nature. He wrote in 1 Thessalonians 5:23: "Now may the God of peace Himself sanctify you completely; and may your whole spirit, soul and body be preserved blameless at the coming of our Lord Jesus Christ." Mankind, being a tripartite being (having three dimensions), experiences this process of transformation in three major areas of his life (See Graph 1). This developmental excursion begins when the rebirth of the spirit of man transpires. The spirit of man in this process is recreated by the Holy Spirit, resulting in man's initial salvation experience (paraphrased John 3:15-17). The soul (mind) of man then goes through the process of transformation and renewal, resulting in conformity to God's ideas and thoughts (paraphrased Romans 12:2). Lastly, the body of man will be changed to an immortal (not subject to death; eternal) state after passing from the physical to the heavenly (1 Corinthians 15:53).

This transformative process should effect and impact the actions and attitudes of believers, culminating in the pre-determined goal of God that believers be "transformed into the image of His Son" (Romans 8:29). The being or the existence of man changes significantly. Thus, this method transforms the whole being of man with the goal of changing the world for God's glory. The Apostle Paul taught the Colossian Christians concerning death:

GRAPH 1. THE HUMAN DIMENSION

SPIRIT	SOUL	BODY
CONSCIOUS	*MIND	FLESH
COMMUNION	WILL	BLOOD
WISDOM	EMOTIONS	BONE
	SELF CONSCIOUNESS	5 SENSES
	INTELLECT/KNOWLEDGE	
	MEMORIES	
	SOCIALIZATION/ENVIRONMENT	
	MENTALIES/MINDSETS	

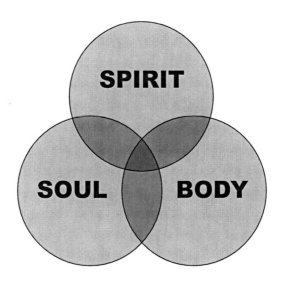

Scriptural References:

Philippians 2:12 ...work out your own soul salvation.

James 1:21 ...receive with meekness the engrafted word which is able to save your souls.

I Corinthians 15:42, 50, 53 ...The Body is sown in corruption, is raised in incorruption...

John 3:16 For God so loved the world...whoever believes in Him should not perish but have everlasting life.

Romans 1:16 For I am not ashamed of the Gospel of Christ for it is the power of God to salvation for everyone who believes.

2 Peter 2:1 I wish above all that you will prosper and be in health, as your soul prospers.

The Human Dimension Continued

*Facts on the Mind
- Nerve center
- Emotional Center
- Mind is located in the soul realm
- Mind/Soul used interchangeably
- Spirit is born again, but the mind has to be renewed

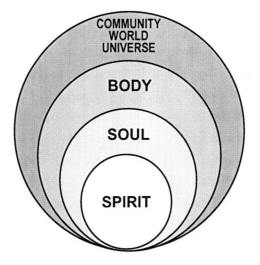

Spirit – Has been saved, born again
Body – Shall be saved, raised incorruptible
Soul – Is being saved, the mind renewed in the Word of God

All human dimensions combined impact the believer's community, world, and universe.

If you died with Christ from the basic principles of the world, why, as though living in the world, do you subject yourselves to regulations—do not touch, do not taste, do not handle, which all concern things which perish with the using—according to the commandments and doctrines of men? These things indeed have an appearance of wisdom in self-imposed religion, false humility, and neglect of the body, but are of no value against the indulgence of the flesh (Colossians 2:20-23)

Paul taught against submission to the world's views. He instructed Christians not to subject themselves to the doctrines of men that do nothing in regard to dying to or denying self-wisdom, self-righteousness, and the desires of the fleshly nature. There has to be a death or subjugation of the man created and indoctrinated by societal culture, principles of the world, and self-imposed religions. There has to be a death to the "self" (selfishness) to which the individual has been disposed and subjected. From the perspective of kingdom consciousness, a believer enters into the process of understanding the truth about himself the way God sees and intends for him to be.

After the born-again experience (spirit salvation), there also is a change in perspective because Kingdom of God consciousness is a revelation of God's mind and thoughts to the individual believer. There comes the great surge of knowing God Himself on a personal basis. The consciousness of man begins to change from self-consciousness (focused on human needs, appetites, and satisfactions) to God-consciousness where there is devotion toward pleasing the

Creator and not pleasing the creation. As a result, the mind changes, therefore actions change. Ultimate divine ("of, like, or from God; Godly," *Webster's College Dictionary*) power comes when the mind is transformed to see as God sees, hear as God hears, and be in the world as God is, creating, exerting power, and subduing for His good pleasure.

Once Kingdom of God consciousness in the believer is elevated to God's belief system the believer develops heavenly perspective about the power and ability of Almighty God. Kingdom consciousness is the catalyst of power to know divine destiny and the authority given to the believer as he lives out his destiny in the earthly realm. On this level of Kingdom consciousness, the power to execute God's divine mandates within one's destiny is realized.

> *Kingdom consciousness is the catalyst of power to know divine destiny and the authority given to the believer as he lives out his destiny in the earthly realm.*

Even heaven and earth are "waiting for the revealing of the sons of God" to walk in this dimension of freedom. The scripture denotes: "For the earnest expectation of the creation eagerly waits for the revealing of the sons of God" (Romans 8:19). The sons of God are those who have received Christ through confession of faith and the progressive transformation of their minds (paraphrased Romans 8:15-17). They understand their divine destinies as heirs of God and

recipients of all God offers in His Kingdom (paraphrased Romans 8:17). These believers experience true awakening to God's perspective about their authority and their ability to transform inwardly, and then they can impact the ideals and opinions of godless generations.

The revealed sons of God who have Kingdom of God consciousness walk in a dimension beyond the limitations of the systems of the world. They receive help from a supernatural source as explained in Ephesians 6:10-12:

> Finally, my brethren, be strong in the Lord and in the power of His might. Put on the whole armor of God that you may be able to stand against the wiles of the devil. For we do not wrestle against flesh and blood but against principalities, against powers, against the rulers of darkness, against the rulers of this age, against spiritual hosts of wickedness in the heavenly places.

There are spiritual dimensions that control the earth's realm, and these sons of God execute authority to stop, demolish, and change these controls by appropriating God's laws and His network of power. God's Kingdom consciousness allows the believer to live in a sphere of executing God's plan in the earth, conquering systems antagonistic to God's intentions, and creating an atmosphere that glorifies and magnifies the true God. This level of awakening is where Kingdom of God consciousness provokes divine action and results.

The Kingdom creates a sphere and a location on earth where the dimension of God's rulership is apparent and functions supernaturally. This is the dimensionality (the scope and magnitude) of Kingdom consciousness. In Genesis 1:26,

God said (during the creation event): "Let Us make man in Our image and according to Our Likeness; let them have dominion over the fish of the sea, over the birds of the air, over the cattle, over all the earth and over every creeping thing that creeps on the earth." Existing in the image and likeness of God, Adam, through obedience, dominated and subdued the dimension that God had established for him. This is the inheritance for all who realize they are sons of God.

A CONSCIOUS BECOMING

This is the reason the enemy of God (Satan) fights believers in God so diligently in the soul realm, man's mental faculties. Of the three dimensions—spirit, soul, and body—the soul realm (which contains the mind) is the dimension being regenerated and restored. The Apostle Paul explained in Romans 12:2 that believers should not be conformed to the world and its mindsets, but be transformed by renewing the mind by the Word of God. The awakening of Kingdom consciousness happens in the soul and mind of man. The Apostle Peter encouraged the church suffering persecution and rejection because of their obedience to Christ: "Gird up the loins of their minds, be sober, and rest hopefully upon the grace that is to be brought to you at the revelation of Jesus Christ" (1 Peter 1:13).

Existing in this life that is apart from the world will engender trouble that must be met with strenuous discipline of the mental faculties. The spiritual battle is lost and won in the context of the mind of men. The Apostle Peter challenged believers to prepare for spiritual action. The first-century Christians had to position themselves in sanctity of God, being like God in conduct and character. The mind, with its ability to comprehend the spiritual part of the self, accommodates this awakening. To fight against it is to keep Kingdom consciousness hidden, inactive, and dead to the workings of God. Our spirit-man knows the truth and is able to discern it.

"Who knows a man except the spirit of the man?" (1 Corinthians 2:11). But to activate and live in the reality of the Kingdom of God is a process which is culminated in

Kingdom of God awareness is not only a belief, but a "becoming" it is the state or condition of progressively attaining God's likeness.

mankind's conscious knowing.

Kingdom of God awareness is not only a belief, but a "becoming;" it is the state or condition of progressively attaining God's likeness. To "be" means to exist, aliveness, and the conscious state; to exist or live (*Webster's College Dictionary*). If the devil can fight the conscious state, which is the part of the human existence where decisions and choices occur, then he can hinder conscious awareness of the Kingdom of God. These hindrances may manifest through malignancies of the soul, body, circumstances, and the cessation of purposeful living.

Consciousness of God's Kingdom is intertwined with human mental and psychological components. God, through

the Holy Spirit, speaks to the spirit of man, which informs man's mind. In the mind, thinking, decision-making, and understanding take place. The Kingdom plan of God is expressed through man's understanding and comprehension (his mental workings). Without the mental and psychological factors there is no realization of Kingdom manifestation. This Kingdom state or consciousness is about the unveiling and revealing to the believer's heart and mind of an unknown world ruled by God. This Kingdom not only has to be known, but also revealed in order to be experienced. It is not traditional church members (those unaffected by a consciousness of God's Kingdom) who walk in the Kingdom dimension; on the contrary, it is knowing, believing, transformed, and faithful sons of God (sonship is a positional inheritance) that have this consciousness.

This Kingdom consciousness is having knowledge of true God-given identity; not the identity the world or culture or family tradition or lies from the enemy have programmed. It is the true identity God has bestowed and intended before conception or even creation occurred. As the Apostle Peter declared in 1 Peter 2:9: "But you are a chosen generation, a royal priesthood, a holy nation, His own special people, that you may proclaim the praises of Him who called you out of darkness into His marvelous light." This is the divine identity of true believers. This Kingdom consciousness is knowing the answers to proverbial human questions: "Why was I created?" and "Why do I exist?"

These are traditional existential questions that have baffled and perplexed the minds of theologians and philosophers from Thomas Aquinas to Aristotle and beyond. Aristotle, a

Greek philosopher and scientist, invented the study of formal logic where logic is purported to be the basic means of reason. The Athenian philosopher believed that the way to truth was natural reason without revelation. He viewed God as distant and unapproachable. Aristotle taught that everything begins in the "sense" realm and moves to abstract thought; therefore, he intellectualized God, declaring that form and matter constitute reality. The philosopher instructed his students to understand that the highest potential for human beings was the development of reason to its fullest capacity.

Thomas Aquinas, a thirteenth-century Catholic philosopher, furthered Aristotle's thinking by bringing Christianity and Aristotelian worldviews systematically together. Aquinas believed in reason; however, he furthered the idea by asserting that faith completes reason without contradicting it. This professor also used logic and reason to prove the existence of God outside of revelation. Aquinas was a Catholic priest as well as one of the most prominent thinkers to bridge a system of theology and philosophy. This systematic theologian believed in revelation and reason. He instructed that the end of man was in the love of God learned only through revelation. Aquinas believed that God was personal and truth incorporated grace and mystery, logic and reason. His body of work is called scholasticism because his methodology forged academic institutions that would later grow into universities.

Man's quest to understand his primeval state of being seems never to be resolved through logic, reason, and systematic ideals. However, the answer is summed up quite simplistically: a revealed Kingdom of God consciousness within the heart of man. This revelation encompasses the answers to all the deep longings and nagging taunts of the human heart.

There are deep longings in the inner depths of every man's heart to know why he exists. The answer comes through a true consciousness of God's Kingdom inside the heart, a true relationship with the revealed God. It is that deep longing and the void that never seems to be filled that drives man toward his orientation in life. It is the tears that flow for no apparent reason and the emptiness that puzzles when nothing and no one can satisfy the cravings of the human heart. Regardless of all the material luxuries of life nothing can fill the place of groaning and the eternal yearning for spiritual fulfillment through God. One cannot "be" who he is divinely destined to be until he knows who he is, perceives why he was created, and understands his purpose in the mind of God.

Kingdom authority is having the mind of God and being awakened to God's principles as this process takes place inside the heart. The culture of God's Kingdom is revealed to the believer through the channel of the believer's mind. This is what every human being longs for. The revelation of God's Kingdom has the innate ability to quench the deep hunger for the eternal God and the eternal spirit of God in every human personality. It cannot be manufactured by machines or by the brilliant minds of men. But Kingdom consciousness is an awakening to true self in the domain of God. Nothing can take its place.

Men try to fill this void with all types of man-constructed products and gadgets. People attempt to deny this eternal longing with everything imaginable, from food to entertainment to ungodly lifestyles of alcohol, drugs, and illicit sexual relations. However, no material or earthly entity can fill this longing because it requires God, who is the spiritual

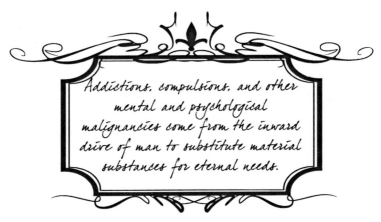

Addictions, compulsions, and other mental and psychological malignancies come from the inward drive of man to substitute material substances for eternal needs.

fulfillment to satisfy the yearning.

One cannot substitute personal outlook for God's perspective. God's Kingdom awareness transports a human view to one that operates on a different level, on the level of a heavenly paradigm. This heavenly paradigm is the perspective of heaven; it is the sphere submitted to the rulership of God.

This is to understand the pattern of how God rules in His spiritual realm of operations. Addictions, compulsions, and other mental and psychological malignancies come from the inward drive of man to substitute material substances for eternal needs. This is the reason more and more man-made substances have to be used increasingly. A person can never be satisfied with the current level of indulgence.

The prophet Ezekiel wrote to the Israelite nation warning them of the total destruction of the city of Jerusalem and the departure of God's presence because of their multiplied acts of harlotry and sin. In the face of continual dissatisfaction in

these relationships, the nation insisted on engaging in the sins of harlotry that reflected distrust in God (paraphrased Ezekiel 16:28-29).

Kingdom awareness is not something to be haphazardly desired; on the contrary, it must be seen as essential—vital to life—as the believer pushes toward the ultimate goal of being like Christ and conforming to His image (paraphrased Romans 8:29). To bring the Kingdom of God to a world oblivious to it one must first "become" the Kingdom, living an existence controlled by God. In order to "become" the Kingdom one must know and understand it. To know the Kingdom of God is to have the truth about it fixed in one's mind. It is to be familiar with the concepts that distinguish God's Kingdom from another. To understand God's Kingdom is to have thorough knowledge of the principles and concepts of God's ruling domain. Understanding brings comprehensive grasp of the significance and the importance of Kingdom awareness as it is progressively and divinely revealed to the heart of every believer. This is the Kingdom of God, a Kingdom of divine consciousness.

The Kingdom of God is a revealed consciousness. It is a mindset seized by the power of a Kingly God for His own purposes in the culmination of an historical, divine plan. One cannot work for an awareness of this magnitude; it has to be unveiled to the mind's understanding.

The Kingdom of God includes the believer in all of his Christ-given glory, arrayed like God in wisdom, strength, dominion, righteousness, and character. Wisdom is true insight into the nature of all things. Wisdom entails the correct application of knowledge. Strength is the inclusion of every aspect of physical, mental, authoritative, and moral power.

Dominion is the territory governed by God's rulership. Righteousness is an attribute of God—uprightness, moral correctness, and imputed justification. Character is the aggregate of features and traits that form the nature of a person; moral and ethical excellence.

Within the process of attaining God consciousness, the believer progressively experiences personal revelation of his true self the way God views him. God views him as His own family, declaring that he is God's son and heir. In Galatians 4:7, the sonship of the believer is iterated: "Therefore you are no longer a slave but a son, and if a son, then an heir of God through Christ." In the context of a natural family, descendents—children by virtue of birth or adoption—receive the inheritance of the parents. Whatever the parents acquire and possess belongs to them. Similarly, being a son or heir of God means to stand as a receiver of all God possesses. God views the believer as one appointed to receive the fullness of His spiritual wealth and blessings (paraphrased Ephesians 1:3).

God's goodness to mankind is that He gave man a conscience and then filled that consciousness with Himself, His thoughts, and His ways to allow man to be like Him in manifesting the Kingdom of God on earth. Therefore, it is recorded in Matthew 6:10: "Your kingdom come. Your will be done, on earth as it is in heaven." God desires that His rule be established not only in the consummation of history, but in our present lives and situations (Hayford 1414). Man's consciousness of the Kingdom of God is God's extension of rulership in the earthly sphere.

For instance, God breathed into Adam the breath of life and he became a living soul (paraphrased Genesis 2:7).

Through this process, the Kingdom extension to earth had been established. God breathed His Spirit into man. God's Spirit contained the entire mind of God, the nature of God, the life and character of God. With all of God's likeness within man, mankind was able to connect with who God was in heaven and express this same rulership on earth. Thus, this process established the extension of God's Kingdom on the earth. Within God's breath was the breath of life—"in Him was life" (John 1:4). God gave man the breath of life that only He could give. He breathed into man's soul and man became alive. Man is a triune being (three dimensional parts) composed of spirit, soul, and body (paraphrased 1Thessalonians 5:23b), and it is in the soul that man's consciousness resides. In the Amplified version of the Bible, Hebrews 4:12 further explains:

> For the word that God speaks is alive and full of power making it alive, and full of power making it active, operative, energizing, and effective; it is sharper than any two-edged sword, penetrating to the dividing line of the breath of life (soul) and the immortal spirit, and of joints and marrow of the deepest part of our nature, exposing and shifting and analyzing and judging the very thoughts and purposes of the heart (Hebrews 4:12).

Also in the soul of man are the mind, will, intellect, emotions, consciousness, memories, mentalities, mindsets, and knowledge. The mind is the central part of the soul. Because the mind occupies such an expansive area of the soul the two terms are sometimes used interchangeably. The mind is the area of the soul that has to be renewed and established in the principles of the Kingdom of God. The will is a component of the soul that facilitates human choice and deliberate actions. To say man is a "free moral agent" is to emphasize the freedom given by God to make choices in life.

The intellect is the function of the mind by which man knows or understands. It is the area capable of thinking and acquiring knowledge. Emotion is the state of the mind where one experiences feelings and sensibilities. Emotions are the opposite of reason. Consciousness is the condition of awareness of the full activity of the mind and senses. Memories are the mental capacity to recall or retain facts, events, impressions, or previous experiences. The mentality of the mind denotes inclination or personal outlook. Mindsets are the fixed attitudes or intentions of the mind. Knowledge is the acquaintance with facts, truths, or principles and is gained through mental apprehension.

It was in the fall of Adam that not only his spirit and body, but also his soul died, being separated from God (paraphrased Genesis 2:17). Adam developed a need to blame, to hide, and to even judge God. In covering and hiding himself, Adam broke from a God-consciousness to a state of self-consciousness (Paraphrased 3:7-10). Before Adam and Eve ate of the forbidden tree they were naked and yet unashamed, focusing their attention on God and walking with Him in the garden.

Separation from God placed the man's attention on himself and created his ruin-giving rise of self-consciousness. Adam covered himself and his wife with fig leaves because of his realization of his nakedness and shame (Genesis 3:10). Shame—suffering disgrace—rendered to Adam an inward perspective about himself. Consequently, his focus was not on

God, but on his own inadequacies.

As a result of disobedience, God's presence, which initially covered Adam, had been removed. Therefore, the process to restore man's broken, self-conscious soul commenced; God's redemptive plan including the sacrifice of Jesus—His death and the offering of his sinless blood—that would eradicate the sin of mankind brought on by Adam's disobedience. The blood of Jesus not only eradicated sin, but also restored the relationship between God and man.

The Kingdom of God dimension is the world of heaven exposed to the human spirit and heart. The Apostle Paul explains in 1 Corinthians 2:10-12:

> But God has revealed them [things God has prepared] to us through His Spirit. For the Spirit searches all things, yes, the deep things of God. For what man knows the things of a man except the spirit of the man which is in him? Even so no one knows the things of God except the Spirit of God. Now we have received not the spirit of the world, but the Spirit who is from God, that we might know the things that have been freely given to us by God.

Those that believe in the redemption brought about through Christ have the Sprit of God dwelling within their human spirits to impart the understanding of God's culture and principles. The Kingdom of God is within every believer's heart, mind, and cognizance. According to the scripture in Luke 17:21 (Amplified): "The Kingdom of God is already within you." The word "already" signifies that the Kingdom of God was placed in man's heart before he knew it was there. This statement presupposes that the Kingdom is there in the

heart, but unknown. Therefore, it has to be revealed to the person. After man receives a born-again spirit thorough faith in Jesus he experiences God through the person of the Holy Spirit moving into his spirit. But progressively, God's Kingdom has to be revealed to man's consciousness and man's mental faculties in order for him to gradually experience all that the Kingdom has to offer.

Consequently, a Kingdom mentality is indispensible to a Kingdom life. The Kingdom of God is a dimension of understanding about God and His ways of rulership in heaven and on earth through every believer. This comprehension about God is then appropriated throughout the person's life, internally and externally. But this Kingdom awareness comes as revelation of knowledge concerning God's Kingdom and its eternal dimensions including rewards for service to God after transition from earth to heaven (paraphrased Revelation 22:12). These eternal dimensions include a Kingdom lifestyle and culture on earth emanating from God's commanded design.

The Kingdom of God is not a heralded message. However, believers, having turned their faces to the Kingdom, become the Kingdom message in the world—the message about belief in Christ whom God sent—and become a witness (duplicate) of Him in the entire world.

The Kingdom-conscious person raises the standard as he lives out his appointed destiny. As Bishop Eddie Long explains in his sermon, "The Real Kingdom": "We are the sanctuary, the marching order. When we leave the church gathering, we then become the Kingdom of God." Believers become the connection between what God demands and man's wake-up call to the divine demand. With the Kingdom perspective, they are appointed to communicate God's Kingdom program to the world. Concurrently, the divine mandate includes a returning back to God, His methodology, and His ways of operating in the earth.

THE HOLY SPIRIT FROM THE BEGINNING

In the Kingdom of God and God's way of doing and being, the mindset is to do and be as God intended, not making an agenda fraught with personal ambitions or concepts apart from Him. This is not a man-conquering feat outside of the living God. Mankind in all of his abilities and physical and mental strength cannot accomplish the Kingdom of God mandate without the assistance of the God who established this Kingdom. After Jesus was resurrected from the dead He showed Himself to His disciples. He "breathed on them and said to them to receive the Holy Spirit" (John 20:22). Jesus imparted the Holy Spirit to the disciples before He ascended back to God in heaven. All who would believe and trust in Christ for the eradication of their sins would receive the Holy Spirit. The aid God gives comes through the power of the Holy Spirit and the revelation of His role in the lives of believers.

The Holy Spirit is the Revealer of truth and the Helper who comes alongside to aid and support. This Personality of the triune Godhead comes alongside to comfort, expose, aid, and minister to the heirs of God's salvation (paraphrased John 16:7, 8 NKJV). The Spirit of God is a part of the inheritance of the Saints. The Spirit gives gifts and helps to light the way through the scriptures that the believer's consciousness and spirit may be illuminated with the truth of God. This process of illumination is not about man's opinions, but the transporting of the mind of God to the minds and hearts of men. As a result of this divine transference, man can then understand his need for God's salvific plan to restore man back to a God-consciousness focus.

In order to have Kingdom of God consciousness awakened in the life of a believer there has to be an empowerment from heaven. Divine help and assistance is needed. The Spirit of Truth, who is referred to by Jesus during His earthly ministry as the Promise or the Helper (Luke 24:49; John 15:26) is the One who aids the believer in his quest to live out the mandates of God. Essentially, God's Spirit is the third personality of the Godhead. "The Holy Spirit, the third Person of the Trinity, proceeds from the Father and is worshiped and glorified together with the Father and the Son. He inspired the scriptures, empowers God's people, and convicts the world of sin" (Hayford 1996).

The definition of the word "spirit" in the Greek, "Parakletos" or Paraclete, is advocate or intercessor, comforter, person called to help or aid (Strong 190). Jesus, after consoling the disciples in His last moments on earth, explained: "Nevertheless I tell you the truth. It is to your advantage that I go away; for if I do not go away, the Helper will not come to you; but if I depart, I will send Him to you" (John 16:7). Sending the Holy Spirit was a part of the spiritual blessing God guarantees as a result of life in Christ (paraphrased 2 Corinthians 1:21-22). The Spirit of Christ can be in the hearts of men in all places, teaching, instructing, and guiding them toward the will of God. The eternal Spirit guides the believer into all truth as He uncovers and teaches God's ways. He also goes along with the believer through continued influences and heightened awareness (Strong 190).

The Holy Spirit is not merely an atmosphere or an aura, but a "Person" of the Godhead (Murdock 3). The Holy Spirit was in the beginning with God and Jesus as God made the world (paraphrased Genesis 1:1, 2). The activity of the Spirit of God was seen in the first book of the Bible, Genesis, where the "Holy Spirit hovered over the face of the waters" (Genesis 1:2). In *Webster's College Dictionary*, the word "hover" means to keep lingering about, waiting near at hand or moving about waiting. The Holy Spirit waited at the hand of God until God spoke the entities of creation into existence. God the Father, Son, and Holy Spirit created the entire universe through the words spoken. The Spirit of God is also the power from heaven as Jesus declared to the disciples before He ascended to the Father: "But you shall receive power after the Holy Spirit has come upon you" (Acts 1:8a). The Holy Spirit is the empowerment of the church for the ministry of the Kingdom of God. Jesus was empowered by the Spirit of God to perform miracles, to preach the Kingdom, and to heal the sick (Matthew 4:23). The church was also authorized by the Holy Spirit to do the same work. The Holy Ghost is the exertion of the power and force of heaven.

The Spirit of God is alluded to in the historical text when, after God made night and day, the heavenly bodies, and the animal and plant kingdoms, He said: "Let Us make man in Our image, according to Our likeness" (Genesis 1:26). God was directly speaking to the rest of the Trinity—Jesus and the

Holy Spirit. Again, the specific order that God gave was to "make" man. Make is a word of action. It is full of creative potential. The Holy Spirit was given the responsibility of sculpting, forming, and shaping the man that God had in mind; a man like God with all the attributes of God including speaking, living, seeing, hearing, creating, thinking, reasoning, and perceiving (Murdock 3-4). Along with Jesus, the Holy Spirit was involved with the creation of man when God declared that They would make and form man according to Their image and likeness.

Another predominate position that the Holy Spirit utilizes is in the poetic book of Proverbs written by King Solomon around 950 B.C. (Hayford 883). The book of Proverbs is full of references to God's Word as the beginning of wisdom. Wisdom was personified in the writings for emphasis, referring to "her spirit" in chapter 1 verse 23. Her spirit logically is the Spirit of God. Wisdom then comes from the Spirit of God or the Holy Spirit. Therefore, the Holy Spirit is wisdom. The Holy Spirit imparts wisdom, reveals wisdom, and illuminates wisdom to the hearts of mankind. Wisdom denotes knowledge of what is true and right coupled with just judgment; it is discernment or insight; sense and understanding; sapience and erudition; a sum of learning through the ages; lasting insight; the capacity to make due use of knowledge (Dictionary.com).

The Holy Spirit takes the raw materials (resources) of knowledge and understanding; then the Spirit constructs a "house" of wisdom. "Through wisdom a house is built, and by understanding it is established" (Proverbs 24:3). The Holy Spirit connects the building blocks of intellect and information to a sound, principled awareness of a thing. Through the wisdom of the Holy Spirit one has the capacity not just for ideas, but to make the ideas work for the masses. Wisdom applies knowledge and insight to produce thorough understanding and skillful judgment.

The Holy Spirit is the wisdom of God transcendent (heavenly, peaceable, pure), beyond earthly wisdom or philosophical knowledge. Without the Holy Spirit of God wisdom would be beyond the reach of mankind in his fallen nature. However, the Holy Spirit is the bridge from the mind of God to the mind of men. "In giving the Holy Spirit, God gives Himself and all that He is" (Murray 10).

> *the Holy Spirit is the bridge from the mind of God to the mind of men.*

THE HOLY SPIRIT IN THE OLD TESTAMENT

When Adam and Eve experienced the fallen state after their disobedience to God, every part of creation fell for the Apostle Paul reminded the Roman Christians how all of creation was subjected to futility and ineffectiveness, but how it, too, would be delivered into the liberty of the children of God (paraphrased Romans 8:20-21). Because of Adam, the ground grew thorns and thistles and he had to "till the ground by the sweat of his brow" (Genesis 3:17, 18), meaning the land was no longer in subjection to him. He had to force it to produce. Eve bore children through hard, painful labor (paraphrased Genesis 3:16). And the arch enemy of God became the arch enemy of humanity—Satan (paraphrased Genesis 3:14-19).

Through his sin Adam lost his position with God and was alienated from Him. Adam no longer had unbroken fellowship with God. He broke the boundaries of God's laws which resulted in separation from God and His Spirit. Through disobedience to God, he became obedient to another voice that became his god. Adam subjected himself not to the Creator, but to the created. However, the worst effect of the fall was the displacement of God's Spirit. Adam lost the Holy Spirit (Munroe 171).

The Holy Spirit was the connector between Adam and the mind of God. The Spirit of God reveals the mind of God and Adam lost that link. He listened to the suggestions of his wife, Eve, who betrayed the divine intent of God (paraphrased Genesis 3:12). Therefore, Adam and all of humanity fell from God's grace (unmerited favor) and the consciousness of God and became conscious of self-initiated thoughts.

It is the Holy Spirit who bridges the gap between human frailty and the omnipotent, all-powerful mind of God. The Holy Spirit, who is from heaven, speaks to every believer the truth that He hears in heaven and declares it to the believer (paraphrased John 16:13-14). Without the Holy Spirit mankind could not know God in His holiness and righteousness. Neither could mankind know or perceive heaven.

The Creator God already had a plan in place to win mankind back to Himself and restore what was lost and given up in the Garden of Eden. God's methodology for the restoration of mankind came through Jesus Christ's sacrificial offering of Himself. Before this ultimate sacrifice would take place, establishing God's plan in the history of mankind, many centuries would pass. Therefore, God set a prototype of His agenda through the nation of Israel before the time of Jesus' earthly ministry. God chose Moses to lead a people He had chosen from the slavery of the Egypt. God had established this people as the ancestral line through which the Messiah would come to open the way for the restoration of the entire human race.

The Holy Spirit was present even in this epoch of God's initial establishment of Israel as a theocracy—the belief in one supreme god as ruler (Musser and Price 274-275)—and spiritual nation for God. Before Moses became Israel's leader he witnessed God's preincarnate presence in a burning bush while shepherding his father-in-law's sheep in the western Arabian city of Midian (paraphrased Genesis 3:2-4). The scriptural text reads: "And the Angel of the Lord appeared to him [Moses] in a flame of fire from the midst of a bush. So he looked, and behold the bush was burning with fire, but the bush was not consumed" (Genesis 3:2). Beside the typical theophany (a deity's manifest presence) of fire used as a sign of God's presence, especially in the Hebrew Scriptures, the "fire" of the burning bush is also a symbol much used for the manifestation of the Holy Spirit and His work in the hearts of men (Laymon 39). The place on the mountain where the Holy Spirit manifested God's presence—Mount Sinai—would be a place of continual sanctuary in Israelite national history.

The presence of the Holy Spirit through the chronicles of Israel's history is witnessed through the ten plagues that came upon Pharaoh and Egypt as Israel transitioned out of four hundred years of forced enslavement. The power of the Holy Spirit rested upon the prophet Moses to perform miraculous wonders (Exodus 4:9): The River Nile was turned into blood.

The Egyptian land and homes were smitten with frogs. Through Aaron, Moses' brother, the dust of Egypt was struck and lice came upon the people and their animals. Thick swarms of flies came into all the land of Egypt. Pestilence came on the beasts of Egypt and all the livestock died. Boils broke out into sores on all the men and beasts of Egypt. Hail mingled with fire came down on the land.

> Moses stretched his rod over the land of Egypt and the east wind blew in the locusts and the land of Egypt was dark with the locust. They ate every green herb and all the fruit left from the hail. Darkness then fell on the land of Egypt. It was so dark that they could not see each other and no one moved from his place for three days (Exodus 10:13-15).

Then at last every first-born in Egypt, from Pharaoh's family to all the servants and people, died.

Although on the surface these plagues or woes might seem moderately random, the Spirit of God had ultimate reasons for choosing those particular warnings. It has been debated that each of these plagues were aimed at the various gods of the Egyptians as well as the Egyptians themselves. Through His Spirit, God exhibited by a show of force that He ruled over the false gods and they were powerless against the One true God.

For instance, the plague of the frogs, it is explained, was a direct attack on the goddess Heqt who the Egyptians believed assisted women in childbirth (Laymon 42). The first three plagues (all the waters of Egypt turning to blood, the plague of the frogs, and the plague of lice) affected everyone, even the

Israelites themselves (Hayford 94). But with the next plagues—
the swarms of flies, the diseased livestock, and the boils on
man and beast—it is believed the Spirit of God distinguished
between Egyptians and Israelites (Hayford 94). Scripture states
the thick swarms of flies were in all of Egypt except in the land
of Goshen where the people of Israel resided (Exodus 8:21-
22). God's deliberate action of allowing the thick swarm of
flies to extend throughout Egypt except for Goshen clearly was
a distinct demonstration of God's power over Egypt and its
gods. Furthermore, this strong exhibition also showed God's
care and kindness for those whom He called His own.

The fifth plague that destroyed the livestock is viewed as an
attack on the mother-goddess Hathor who was portrayed in
the form of a cow in which the Egyptians worshipped (Laymon
43). Hathor was the cow-headed goddess of love, joy, woman,
childbirth, and music (McDevitt "Ancient Egypt: the
Mythology"). As early as the eleventh century it is said that the
Egyptians believed she was important because when a child
was born seven Hathors came to the child's bedside to decide
the infant's future (McDevitt).

The miracle of hail was an abnormal phenomenon to the
Egyptians because hail rarely occurs in the desert. The Spirit of
God was moving in such as way as to alert the people that God
had power over the natural world. The plagues of the hail, boils,
and locusts have been regarded as an assault on ancient Egypt's
worship of the goddess of life and the protector of harvests.

According to writer and theologian Jack Hayford,
regarding the plagues of Egypt:

The ninth plague that entailed darkness is said to have a
two-fold meaning as to why the Spirit of God

promulgated such a demonstration of His sovereignty. The first meaning referred to an attack on the symbol of the sun which, in Egyptian culture, is considered the most powerful relic (Hayford 97).

In this particular plague, the Spirit of God illustrated God's dominance over the sun. It is also thought he darkening of the sun was God's way of demonstrating His attack on the Pharaoh of Egypt, Ramses II, who had established himself as the incarnation of the sun god Amon-Ra (Gottwald, 191). This plague of darkness, as well as the destruction of the first-born in all the land, again illustrated that the Creator-God, through His Spirit, is the one true God and that He has complete power and control over heaven and earth, death and life.

These plagues were a testimony not only to Egypt and its gods, but also to the Israelite nation. Israel had been bombarded for over 400 years with the culture of Egypt including its religious paganism. The Spirit of God, through these demonstrative events in Egypt, began the reprogramming of Israel to the mindset of having one God with all power (Laymon 41). This religious and philosophical thought is called theism, the belief in one God as creator and ruler of the universe (*Webster's College Dictionary*). Through these supernatural occurrences the Holy Spirit initiated the process of changing the minds of the people toward the truth. God began to establish His preeminent place in the lives of the Hebrews and He began to educate them in His ways and culture, beginning with His powerful execution of the plagues of Egypt.

Any time there are displays of miracles, signs, and wonders

from heaven in the scriptural text it is safe to say that the Holy Spirit is present and at work. Taking the nation through the Red Sea or the Sea of Reeds—a narrow body of water that stretches about 1,300 miles from Suez to the Gulf of Aden and has a depth of 9,500 feet—the Holy Spirit displayed another miraculous wonder. The Hebrews crossed on dry ground as the waters were miraculously opened for them. However, for Pharaoh and his army the outcome was catastrophic. When they tried to cross the sea, the waters crashed in, thus destroying every one of them. According to Exodus 14:27b-28: "So the Lord overthrew the Egyptians in the midst of the sea.

Then the waters returned and covered the chariots, the horsemen and all the army of Pharaoh that came into the sea after them. Not so much as one of them remained."

There were many other such miraculous occurrences for Moses and the newly released nation of Israelites that followed their release from slavery. "Then the Lord said to Moses: Behold I will rain down bread from heaven for you..." (Exodus 16:4). Manna or bread was sent from heaven to feed the wandering nation. Also, to quench their thirst, water from the rock was miraculously supplied as they journeyed through the Wilderness of Sin. God declared to Moses: "Behold, I will stand before you on the rock in Horeb; and you shall strike the rock, and water will come out of it, that the people might drink" (Exodus 17: 6). The work of the Holy Spirit in their journey is further demonstrated by all the face-to-face conferences between God and Moses, as well as the presence of God in the form of the glory cloud that covered and filled the tabernacle of meeting. "Moses was not able to enter the tabernacle because the cloud rested above it, and the glory of the Lord filled the tabernacle" (Exodus 40:34).

Another example of the Holy Spirit in the first testament of Holy Scripture was in the lives and ministries of the prophets Elijah and Elisha. The prophet Elijah was raised up during the reign of Ahab, King of Northern Israel about 874-853 B.C. after the reign of Omri his father (1Kings 16:28-29). Ahab walked in the "sins" of Jeroboam who provoked Israel to commit rebellion against God through the worship of idols. The seventh King of Israel, Ahab built a wooden image the Canaanite goddess Asherah in Samaria. 1 Kings 16:33 records God's anger: "And Ahab made a wooden image. Ahab did more to provoke the Lord God of Israel to anger than all the kings of Israel who were before him." God considered Ahab a wicked king because of his insistence in leading Israel to worship idols.

Ahab had married the Sidonian princess, Jezebel, who he was forbidden to marry because of her culture of worshipping Baal, a Phoenician deity (Strong 42)—translated "master" or "lord." Jezebel was the false prophetess who seduced the nation of Israel and Ahab into worshipping Baal instead of Yahweh, "the ineffable name that the Hebrew nation ascribed to God which cannot and should not be expressed in spoken words; YHWH" (Dictionary.com). According to an article in the Interpreter's One-Volume Commentary on the Bible written by a contributing theologian: "Because of the influence of Jezebel, Baalism became established in Samaria as an officially approved cult" during the reign of Ahab (Laymon 192-193).

Elijah, whose name means "Yahweh is God" (Laymon 193), was raised up in direct opposition to the worship of Baal. Many miracles through the Holy Spirit surrounded the life of

Elijah. In 1 Kings 17:1, Elijah was used by the Holy Spirit to demonstrate one of these supernatural occurrences: "And Elijah the Tishbite, of the inhabitants of Gilead, said the Ahab, as the Lord God of Israel lives, before whom I stand, there shall not be dew nor rain these years, except at my word." The significance of this prophecy of no rain is apparent when it is understood that those who worshipped Baal believed that he controlled the rain (Hayford 513). In effect, Elijah condemned Baalism and challenged the worshippers of Baal, "proclaiming that the Lord of Israel controlled the weather" (Hayford 513). As a result, Israel experienced a three-year drought. In 1 Kings 17:2-3, Elijah was instructed by the Holy Spirit to leave the place: "Then the word of the Lord came to him saying, get away from here and turn eastward, and hide by the Brook Cherith, which flows into the Jordan."

The prophet was commanded to go to a certain Brook Cherith where the Holy Spirit would supernaturally provide food for him. Each morning ravens would deliver it and he would have a continuous supply of water from the brook (paraphrased 1 Kings 17:6). In this we understand that God did not leave the prophet in the hands of a wicked king, but sent him to a desert place not under Ahab's jurisdiction. This place of wild ravines near the Jordan River would serve as a secure asylum for the prophet because no one could look for him there.

As a result of the drought God allowed the brook to dry up, but He sent the Holy Spirit with a word of further instruction: "Then the word of the Lord came to him saying, Arise go to Zarephath which belongs to Sidon and dwell there. See I have commanded a widow there to provide for you" (1

Kings 17:9). In obedience, Elijah went as commanded. Because of the drought, the poor widow had little sustenance to aid the prophet. She gave what she had—her last bit of food—and Elijah gave what he had—a word from God. The Holy Spirit performed supernaturally because they were supplied with food throughout the rest of the famine. The ascribed author of 1 Kings, the prophet Jeremiah, eloquently described this supernatural event: "The bin of flour was not used up, nor did the jar of oil run dry, according to the Word of the Lord which he spoke by Elijah" (1 Kings 17:16).

The Holy Spirit performed another miracle by the hands of Elijah. He raised the widow's son from the chambers of death (paraphrased 1 Kings 17:21-23). The son had a grievous sickness that took away his breath. Some surmise that it derived from the weakened state of the child by malnutrition as a result of the famine and previous poverty conditions (Patterson and Austel 136-140). Also, in that time period being a widow with a child was the lowest on the socio-economic scale because she had no husband to care for her. Her only hope was to call on the prophet who earlier had been utilized by God to bring sustenance even in famine. The widow regained hope when the miracle transpired: "Then the Lord heard the voice of Elijah; and the soul of the child came back to him, and he revived" (1 Kings 17:17-22).

At the close of the drought another miracle executed through the Holy Spirit by the hands of Elijah occurred. The looming question of whether it was the Lord of Israel or Baal who controlled the rain and all the conditions of nature was about to be answered. Elijah resurfaced, this time face-to-face with King Ahab. During the meeting, Elijah ordered a decisive demonstration between the power of the god Baal and the power of the Creator God, Yahweh. The prophet ordered:

> "Now therefore send and gather all Israel to me on Mount Carmel, the four hundred and fifty prophets of Baal, and the four hundred prophets of Asherah, who eat at Jezebel's table" (1 Kings 18:19).

Mount Carmel was significant in that the Canaanites built sanctuaries to pagan weather deities. This was the ideal place to show the superiority of the Lord of Israel over Baal. Though the pagan prophets prayed for many hours, there was no response from Baal. However, at the time of the evening sacrifice (about 3:00 P.M.) Elijah built an altar and surrounded it with much water because whoever was God had to answer by burning up the altar. When the prophet Elijah prayed to the God of Israel He sent the fire and consumed the sacrifice.

Even in the drought, Elijah was convinced of his God's omnipotence. The people who had gathered to witness the wonder rendered their verdict: "The Lord, He is God! The Lord, He is God" (1 Kings 18:39). Thus, Elijah's name was fulfilled: "Yahweh is God." The prophet ordered that the prophets of Baal be executed, and not many days following, the rains descended, ending the drought (1 Kings 18:45).

The Holy Spirit remained active in the lives of the prophets during the evolving of the nation of Israel. Miracles occurred throughout the life of Elijah until God took him from the earth supernaturally. God wanted to demonstrate to His people His plan and model of salvation that would come through the nation's lineage in the person of Jesus Christ. The people of Israel stood as an example to surrounding nations as a nation called out and set aside for God's Kingdom plans. Because of the laws that the nation of Israel were required to keep and the worship of only one God in the midst of polytheistic cultures, Israel was vastly different from the surrounding nations and found itself in many precarious situations requiring the aid of God's Spirit. God demonstrated His superior power to Israel by supernatural acts performed upon the surrounding heathen nations as a way of changing their minds about who was really God of the universe.

For example, the prophet Elisha, successor of Elijah, was empowered by the Holy Spirit to administer healing from leprosy to a commander of the Syrian army (paraphrased 2 Kings 5:14). This door of God's demonstration of His healing power was opened to show God's willingness to restore hope to those afflicted who would submit to His process of healing. Naaman, the Syrian general, reluctantly followed the prophet's words to dip in the Jordan River and accordingly his healing manifested. Furthermore, this story parallels what happens to those who come to Jesus for salvation and vindication. Jesus will not turn them away. He expressed His divine love for people through the supernatural demonstration of the Holy Spirit's power of healing: "When the sun was setting, all those who had any that were sick with various diseases brought them to Him; and He laid His hands on every one of them and healed them (Luke 4:40).

POWER FROM THE KINGDOM OF GOD

Jesus Christ—the anointed One of God—came supernaturally and legally into the world of men through the assistance of the Holy Spirit. To come legally into the earth required a human body. Because of God's divine love for humanity, He made Himself human in the person of Christ. Jesus was the incarnate God in human form (Musser and Price 251). In His incarnation, God confirmed His self-involvement with the plight of mankind's suffering and impending death. Because of the fall of Adam God had already coordinated a plan of redemption through the atoning sacrifice of Jesus (paraphrased Romans 5:18, 19), reconciling sinners with God through the cross. Jesus, the second Personality of the God-Head, had to have sin-free blood in order to serve as the sacrificial Lamb of God to remit sins (because all human blood after the fall of Adam was inundated with sin).

Man's blood was tainted with the sin of his forefather, Adam; therefore, no man could bear the burden of sin's penalty. However, Jesus was born of a virgin woman through the seed of the Holy Spirit. The genetic makeup of all man's DNA comes through the blood of the parents ("Genetics and Heredity"). As explained by *Webster's College Dictionary*, DNA or deoxyribonucleic acid is the double-stranded macromolecule of chromosomes that is the material that transfers genetic characteristics in all life forms. The mother only supplies the ovum, the egg. In the case of the birth of Jesus, the Holy Spirit supplied the blood or the DNA. In the Gospel of Luke, this process was unveiled: "And the angel answered and said to her, the Holy Spirit will come upon you, and the power of the Highest will overshadow you; therefore, also the Holy One who is to be born will be called the Son of God" (Luke 1:35). This fusion of both the genetic material from the mother and the pure blood of the Holy Spirit created a body and heavenly blood for God to exist in the material world. The mother of Jesus, Mary, surrendered her body to create the mortal flesh of Jesus; concurrently, the Holy Spirit supplied the DNA in order to create the untainted blood of Jesus. This process created God in man and gives life to the truth that Jesus, although all human, was also all God—living and existing in the same body.

Consequently, even the birth of the Messiah was a supernatural phenomenon spearheaded by Father-God and executed through the Holy Spirit-God. This phenomenon suggested to Mary that the child would have a unique nature.

"The conception of Jesus took place through the direct action of the Holy Spirit" (Hayford 1509). The word "overshadowed" according to *Strong's Exhaustive Concordance of the Bible* means "to cast a shade upon, to envelope in a haze of brilliancy, to invest with preternatural influence. The Holy Spirit exerted creative energy upon the womb of the Virgin Mary impregnating it." This is the same word used in Exodus 40:34-35 when God filled the tabernacle of meeting with His presence and Moses could not enter because the glory cloud covered or *overshadowed* the tabernacle.

The creative force of the Holy Spirit was strongly evident in the ministry of Jesus as the Spirit of God's force was the available power from the Kingdom for the believer in the divine

> Without the workings of the Holy Spirit's activity in the life of mankind a consciousness of God's realm could not be recognized.

quest to express God's plan on earth. The power of God is available to live life in the consciousness of the Kingdom that would express God's presence in the world. The Holy Spirit's working is divine validation of the appearance of Jesus and the emerging church in the New Testament. Without the workings of the Holy Spirit's activity in the life of mankind a consciousness of God's realm could not be recognized.

Jesus, in His earthly ministry, was connected with the power of God: "And the Holy Spirit descended in bodily form like a dove upon Him, and a voice came from heaven which said, You are my beloved Son, in you I am well pleased" (Luke 3:22). The Holy Spirit's role after Jesus was baptized was that anointing—an empowerment to perform a task or complete a job. Jesus was anointed to begin His work and ministry on earth empowered by the Holy Spirit. Before that time, there was no recording of Jesus performing any miracles. However, after He was baptized (fulfilling all righteousness) the Holy Spirit appeared as a manifested sign which anointed Jesus for service and also served as a symbol for Jesus' entrance into His ministry. Luke 4:14 points to Jesus' beginnings of ministering in the power of the Spirit: "Then Jesus returned in the power of the Spirit to Galilee, and the news of Him went out through all the surrounding region." Therefore, the Spirit is intrinsic to the fulfillment of the divine purposes of God for Jesus and for the church.

The Messiah knew that the plan of God was for Him to die on the cross, but He also understood that the Holy Spirit would come to continue the revelation of Jesus in the church age. Jesus explained to his followers: "But when the Helper [Spirit of God] comes, whom I shall send to you from the

Father, the Spirit of truth who proceeds from the Father, He will testify of Me" (John 15:26). Jesus consistently taught His disciples that He would return to the Father so that the Promised Holy Spirit would come and the Spirit of God would rest in the hearts of all believers to teach them the way of the Father. Jesus was empowered by the Holy Spirit to complete His task on earth by dying for the sins of men. He was sinless, yet He became the sacrificial Lamb of God for the redemption of mankind from the world of darkness.

It was the creative force of the Holy Spirit that raised Jesus from the dead and endued Him with all power in heaven and earth (Hayford 1612). Before Jesus went back to heaven, He gave instructions to His disciples and followers: "Behold I send the Promise of My Father upon you, but tarry in the city of Jerusalem until you are endued with power from on high" (Luke 24:49). The Spirit of God was sent to the believers as Jesus had promised during the annual Jewish season of festivals called Pentecost. As required by Jewish law, the men were to go to Jerusalem three times per year to celebrate major feasts— Passover in the spring; Pentecost (meaning fifty) seven weeks and a day later; and Tabernacles in the fall at the end of harvest (Deuteronomy 16:16).

On the day of Pentecost the Holy Spirit was released supernaturally: "When the Day of Pentecost had fully come, they were all in one accord in one place. And they were all filled with the Holy Spirit and began to speak with other tongues, as the Spirit gave them utterance" (Acts 2:1, 4). Because Pentecost was the celebration of first fruits of the harvest season these and others who became Christians (Christ followers) on Pentecost were the first fruits of an immeasurable harvest of souls for God's Kingdom. After the ministry of Jesus the Holy Spirit, as the initial expression of God's new epoch, was dispersed into the hearts of men to fulfill God's divine intent of empowering the church. The Holy Spirit is the Spirit of Truth who continues the revelation of Jesus to the believers in the church age.

THE HOLY SPIRIT AFTER JESUS' MINISTRY

The role of the Spirit of God in the new church age focused the believers continuously on the way of Christ and the Kingdom of God in the world. The church could imitate the same supernatural activities now that the Holy Spirit was with them and "inside" of them in the world. This was a great paradigmatic revolution in the concept of God's power residing "inside" believers.

For example, after the miraculous growth of the church in the book of The Acts of the Apostles, Peter and John went to the temple at the hour of prayer and a lame man asked for alms, donations of charity. Peter looked intently at the man and said: "Silver and gold I do not have, but what I do have I give to you; in the name of Jesus Christ of Nazareth, rise up and walk. And he took him by the right hand and lifted him up, and immediately his feet and ankle bones received strength" (Acts 3:6-7). The man stood up and walked; he went leaping into the temple, praising God. The people realized what had happened and were astonished.

Peter and John gave the lame man what they possessed—the Power of the Holy Ghost. The Spirit of God was on the inside of them evoking heavenly occurrences in the earthly realm, fulfilling the prayer that Jesus taught them: "Our Father in heaven, hallowed be Your name. Your kingdom come. Your will be done on earth as it is in heaven" (Luke 11:2). The Holy Spirit was bringing the rulership of God into the lives of mankind that the inhabitants of the earth could experience the dominion of God over sicknesses and diseases.

The Spirit began to teach believers and impart to them the consciousness of heaven and how to use heavenly power through cooperation with God's Spirit. This cooperation included a surrendering of previous ways of life that did not reflect God's nature and character. Many in that time were astonished at the bold demonstrations of the Holy Spirit's power. According to the Apostle Paul's writings in the book of The Acts of the Apostles, some witnessed the death of Ananias and his wife, Sapphira, when they lied to the Holy Spirit concerning the sale of certain property (paraphrased Acts 5:1-10). Their blatant disregard for the holiness of the Spirit through the apostles warranted a punishment—even death—that would help to establish the Spirit's authority in the local church. This display of power also helped the local church understand the importance of not tolerating acts of deceit and established a high esteem for accountability.

Another personality in the beginning years of the church was Paul (Saul before his conversion experience), a citizen of the country of Cilicia (Hayford 1639). This man had been a persecutor of the church of Jesus Christ, regarding it as a cult or a fascist, separatist party spouting anti-Jewish hypocrisy. However, after his Damascus-Road encounter with the Spirit of Christ, Paul was converted and followed the very person he had previously opposed (paraphrased Acts 9:4-9). After he was miraculously healed of blindness at the hand of Ananias, a disciple and follower of Jesus, Paul was filled with the Holy Spirit and "immediately began to preach the Christ in the synagogues, that He is the Son of God" (Acts 9:20). Because the Holy Spirit revolutionized the inside of Paul, he began, through the Spirit's power, to perform many miracles. He wrote inspirationally to various churches about the truths of God concerning Jesus Christ.

Throughout his ministry, Paul received mighty revelations of the plan of God through the Holy Spirit. He was able to communicate the gospel in such a way that the dispensation of the Holy Spirit would be palpable to the Jewish populace as well as to gentile converts. The Holy Spirit gave Paul a revelation of the "Body of Christ" being the church, having many members with differing functions (paraphrased Romans 12:4, 5). The Apostle explained that all these functions were given by the Holy Spirit to support the work of the gospel (Romans 12:4-8). Paul also explained such topics as the marriage of Christ, spiritual warfare, the armor of God, Godly love, the institution of the Lord's Supper, Jesus as the great High Priest, spiritual gifts, the fruit of the Spirit, the resurrection of the righteous, and many other profound theological topics. Paul was such a force for the establishing of the first-century church that over two-thirds of the New Testament consisted of his divinely-inspired teachings.

Paul preached all over Europe, spreading the gospel, the truth about Christ, and performing miracles and wonders by the power of the Holy Spirit. Through his extraordinary ministry many people believed that Jesus was the Son of God and were saved from their sins. Paul started out as a persecutor of the church of Jesus Christ, but after his revolutionary change through his encounter with the Spirit of God Paul became the premiere vessel through which the gospel was preached, written, and demonstrated.

HOLY SPIRIT CONSCIOUSNESS

The Spirit of God imparts the mind of God and Christ to the church. 1 Corinthians 2:11b states: "Even so no one knows the things of God except the Spirit of God." It is the Holy Spirit who reveals the mind of God to the believer. The Spirit's role is to connect heaven to the mind of those who believe in God in order to express God's will in the earth. Therefore, the heavenly consciousness needed to continue the believer's destiny is inevitably tied to this connection with the Sprit of God.

Without the Holy Spirit's teachings that directly oppose the world's consciousness even the believer could not live a life pleasing to God. The believer would not be any different from Adam and Eve in their selfishness of desire. Selfishness comes from the mindset that places emphasis on what the individual desires and being concerned primarily with one's own interests (Dictionary.com). Selfishness is what the individual wants as opposed to what God wants.

For instance, Eve in the Garden of Eden did not want the commandment of God; she wanted what appealed to her delights. The text uncovers that "when the woman saw that the tree was good for food, that it was pleasant to the eyes, and desirable to make one wise, she took the fruit and ate" (Genesis 1:6). Regardless of what was said by God concerning the command not to eat the fruit she concluded with her reasoning to take the fruit and eat it. In Eve's selfishness and disobedience she made her idea, not God's, the primary law.

Eve supplanted God's law with her desires. The lens through which Eve—and invariable all mankind—sees is personal desire.

The consequences of this disobedience are human limitations and error. Human limitations manifest in the form of disease, classism, prejudice, sin, lawlessness, tyrannical government, misconception, inequity, social ills, inhumane social structures, and greed. The spirit of man is broken and persists in a direction that goes further and further away from the Divine, the ultimate truth. Therefore, the work and the production of mankind, his ideals, and his perceptions emanate from this dysfunctional place within his heart that breeds deficiency. Even if the idea starts with a seemingly selfless motivation it can yet end up destroying and compromising the intended purpose, leaving much collateral damage in its wake. To reiterate, man's awareness of himself and his social world comes from this place of limitations and inadequacy.

To bridge the gap between what man became, his position in the world, and what God desired him to be—his heavenly position—God sent His Son in bodily form—Jesus Christ—to pay the price to restore him to his divine position in the heavenly sphere. Jesus paid the penalty through the cross; furthermore, it is the Holy Spirit who bridges the gap between the heavenly positioning and the earthly experience. As Myles Monroe explains in his book, The Most Important Person on Earth, "The new birth, or conversion, prepares us for heaven.

The baptism of the Holy Spirit, on the other hand, prepares us for earth" (Monroe 157). The Holy Spirit is the One who orchestrates the earthly experience of the believer toward a Kingdom of God consciousness.

When a person accepts God's plan of salvation through Jesus Christ his spirit is reborn through the Spirit of God (paraphrased John 3:16). According to Romans 10:9: "...if you confess with your mouth the Lord Jesus and believe in your heart that God has raised Him from the dead, you will be saved." After a man believes in Jesus, God's Spirit comes to reside in his spirit. This is the restoration of man's broken, fallen spirit. The Holy Spirit comes into the human spirit to guide toward a consciousness of God and His nature. The new birth restores man to his heavenly position, which is a right relationship with God, and the man receives the person of the Holy Spirit.

The indwelling Spirit of God comes to change the perspective of man to the perspective of God and make him fully aware of God's thoughts, plans, and will. It is God making His home in the spirit of the believer. 1 Corinthians 3:16 (Amplified) teaches: "Do you not discern and understand that you [the whole church at Corinth] are God's temple (His sanctuary), and that God's Spirit has His permanent dwelling in you—to be at home in you [collectively as a church and also individually]?" The indwelling Holy Spirit comes when one is born again. Then God's word, through the Holy Spirit, informs man of his place in God's scheme of creation and helps change man's illusionary concept of himself to the truth of what God intended him to be.

Through salvation, the Holy Spirit renders to mankind the power to change from consciousness of darkness to consciousness of light; from "the kingdom of darkness into the Kingdom of God's dear Son" (1 Peter 2:9). The Holy Spirit is the power from God to accomplish the will of God in the inner man as well as the change-agent in the earth. A change-agent is one submitted to God and used by God to bring the Kingdom of God on the earth.

Christ admonished the disciples to stay in Jerusalem until they would receive "power" when the Holy Spirit was released. According to *Strong's Exhaustive Concordance of the Bible*, The Greek word "power" in this context is "dunamis" or miraculous power. Dunamis is the source of the word dynamite. It means force, mighty work, strength. The Holy Spirit is power in the life of the believer to be transformed from one level to the next, to manifest the actions and plans of God in the earth.

It is the Holy Spirit who has been given the job of not only helping the believer to know his positional rights as righteous through the cross of Christ, but also to help the believer live the life of sanctification: "That He might sanctify and cleanse her with the washing of water by the word" (Ephesians 5:26). Sanctification is a life set apart for God. It is the manifestation of a life produced by the indwelling Spirit of God.

Believers are called to live in Christ above the life of the world's making. In 1 John 2:15, believers are admonished: "Do not love the world or the things in the world. If anyone loves the world, the love of the Father is not in him." God is opposed to the life that reflects cooperation with the world and is inundated by the systems of the world which are against the authority of God. Believers are set aside for God's purposes and are distinguished from the world because the world's ways are antithetical to the methods and purposes of God. It is belief in the truth of God that separates the believer from the world (paraphrased 2 Thessalonians 2:13). This life that is set apart from the world and sanctified to God helps the believer become a witness to the truth of God so that the world might believe and desire God's ways. In this process, the believer is empowered through the Holy Spirit to extend the Kingdom of God to those the believer encounters.

> Sanctification includes: freeing from the grip of sin, bringing death (or an end) to the sinful nature of mankind, and manifesting the nature of God in everyday living. Sanctification is then "the dedicated consecration to God, His work and will" (Horton 170).

This process is the work and manifestation of the Holy Spirit.

THE FRUIT AND THE GIFTS OF THE HOLY SPIRIT

The current work of the Holy Spirit in the church age is the continuation of the revelation of Christ on the earth through the process of transforming the mind of the believer.

The Apostle Paul used the example of Christ to establish how believers should conduct themselves: "Let this mind be in you which was also in Christ Jesus" (Philippians 2:5). Paul exhorted people to have their minds

The current work of the Holy Spirit in the church age is the continuation of the revelation of Christ on the earth through the process of transforming the mind of the believer.

and patterns of thinking commensurate with the nature and character of Christ. Five years earlier, his instructions to the Christians in Rome were to be changed in their thinking: "And do not be conformed to this world, but be transformed by the renewing of your mind , that you may prove what is that good and acceptable and perfect will of God" (Romans 12:2).

The apostle established the requirement to be like Christ and to think like Christ. In order to accomplish this, there must be a change in the believer's mental activity. This comes when the believer submits to the indwelling work of the Spirit of God. The Spirit alters the believer's attitudes and character by reprogramming his consciousness to replicate God's attributes as portrayed by the fruit of the Spirit which every believer is instructed to grow and develop. The believer has to move into the consciousness of reflecting God's nature and how God operates in the world. The task of God's Spirit is to bring the believer into this realm of being in which the Kingdom of God is demonstrated by the Godlike character and nature of the believer.

As has been shown, the Holy Spirit is a "Person" of the Godhead. He talks, thinks, plans, and is articulate. He is the voice of the Godhead to the believer. The beloved disciple, John, recorded in the scriptural text: "He [Holy Spirit] shall not speak of Himself; but whatsoever He shall hear, that shall He speak" (John 16:13). The Holy Spirit can enter a life like refreshing water; He can alter a failing life like a refiner's fire; He can move suddenly and quickly like wind. The Holy Spirit is an advisor, a healer, a comforter, and a mentor. He desires to impart His wisdom, His life, and His energy into all who will accept Him. He is the Presence of God to the believer today. He is the revealer of truth and He leads every believer into their testing season.

For example, He led Jesus into his wilderness of testing: "And Jesus was led by the Spirit into the wilderness, being forty days tempted of the devil" (Luke 4:1-2). In addition, it is the Holy Spirit who empowers the believer after the tests are completed: "Then Jesus returned in the power of the Spirit to Galilee, and the news of Him went out through all the surrounding region" (Luke 4:14).

The Holy Spirit is vastly important to the life that has to transition from a consciousness of the world to a consciousness of God's Kingdom. He is the heavenly sphere that settles into the hearts of men to impart the culture of heaven. The Holy Spirit is God "inside" the hearts of men, "seeing something not seen; taking the believer to places they have never been, and planting seeds of what they are becoming. He is the Spirit of Prophecy who brings the future into the heart, for the future has to move into the heart before one can move into their future" (Murdock 19).

It was the Holy Spirit whose breath made the "formed" man live, for the scriptural text described man's creation thus: "And the Lord formed man from the dust of the ground, and breathed into his nostrils the breath of life, and man became a living [breathing, speaking] being [like God]" (Genesis 2:7). Before the man became alive, he was formed, but lifeless. He had a body, but no spirit or soul. Then the creative power of God sent His breath through the man, and then man lived! He could breath, speak, and walk. The power of the Spirit of God created the man to be like God. The Greek word "spirit" in this context is "pneuma," the root of the words "pneumonia," "pneumatology," or "pneumatic" (Strong 205). In the English language, these words mean breath, breeze, a current of air, or wind. According to author Jack Hayford in his book, *People of the Spirit*: "Pneuma is that part of a person capable of responding to God" (Hayford 14).

In the life of every believer the transition from the world's mindsets and ways will ultimately occur. It is impossible to experience the culture of the Kingdom of heaven if one does not experience the inner characteristics of God—His nature and character. This process is not about what God does, but who He is. It is the Holy Spirit who directs and orchestrates this process of sanctification and character development. Furthermore, it is the Holy Spirit who has the function of imparting the holiness of God to every believer.

Without the help and teaching of the Holy Spirit, mankind would not ever, on his own, possess the ability to be like God. It takes the "dunamis" (power) of the Holy Spirit working in each believer for the change God requires (Hayford 1780). This is a supernatural, God-directed process.

> When the Holy Spirit comes into the heart He brings everything necessary for the person to become like the Divine.

When one is born again, God expects the person to gradually become like Him, supporting the attributes of God's nature and character. When the Holy Spirit comes into the heart He brings everything necessary for the person to become like the Divine. This result of the inner working of the Holy Spirit is called the fruit of the Spirit. "As we bear the fruit of the Spirit in our lives, others will see in us the family likeness of God's Son and be attracted to the Savior" (Graham 363). The fruit of the Spirit inevitably resides in every believer; however, the process of developing and manifesting the fruit is the responsibility of the individual with the aid of the Holy Spirit.

One cannot bear spiritual fruit outside of the ministry of the Holy Spirit. Jesus taught His disciples about the vine and bearing fruit:

> Abide in Me, and I in you. As the branch cannot bear fruit of itself, unless it abides in the vine, neither can you unless you abide in Me. I am the vine, you are the branches. He who abides in Me, and I in him, bears much fruit; for without Me you can do nothing (John 15:4, 5).

Jesus also taught that "you will know [judge] them by their fruit" (Matthew 7:20). Therefore, according to God's requirement, the fruit of the Spirit is not only important to develop, but necessary to possess.

In the book of Galatians, the Apostle Paul investigates the liberty of believers in Christ who walk not after the ancient Jewish laws and customs, but who walk in the Spirit. This letter addressed the group of churches in Galatia and was written as a contradiction to the Judaizers (legalists in the church) who called Paul inferior to the apostles James and Peter (Laymon 832). They viewed Paul as a compromiser and believed new converts (Gentile believers) needed to adhere to Jewish laws and customs. This doctrine contradicted the grace of salvation through faith that Paul vehemently taught. However, Paul repudiated their erroneous "works doctrine" by teaching the dynamics of the fruit of the Spirit:

> But if you are led by the Spirit, you are not under the law. But the fruit of the Spirit is love, joy, peace, longsuffering, kindness, goodness, faithfulness, gentleness, self-control. Against such there is no law (Galatians 5:18, 22, 23).

The Holy Spirit leads the believer into the process of becoming like Christ in nature and character. The Apostle Paul's letter to the Ephesians reiterates this point: "Instead we will speak the truth in love, growing in every way more and more like Christ, who is the head of his body the church" (Ephesians 4:15 New Living Translation). Believers are required to operate within the Kingdom of God in the world as Christ had done. This inner process starts with cultivating the fruit of God's Spirit so that believers may reflect God's consciousness in thoughts and actions.

The first cluster of fruit, or triad of grace, deals with love, joy, and peace. These are concerned with the believer's attitude toward God. This first category reflects the believer's relationship with God. The second triad of grace—patience, kindness, and goodness—involves the Christian's social relationships; attitudes portrayed toward others. The third triad of grace is faithfulness, gentleness, and self-control, which entails an inward relationship, or the attitudes and actions of the inner self.

LOVE

Love is the kind of affection God showed at Calvary's cross when Jesus gave His life as a sacrifice for all mankind. This love does not come through the thoughts and ideas of men, nor is it born of an inventive concoction from the brilliance of men's ingenuity. This love is *agape* love; it is born from God and is God. This love will never fail and never cease because it is ultimately who God is. Actually, love is the whole fruit of the Spirit and the rest are descriptions of what love looks like when it is manifested (Hayford 1780). This is that love as described by the beloved disciple, John: "For God so loved the world that He gave His only begotten Son, that whoever believes in Him should not perish but have everlasting life" (John 3:16).

Strong's Exhaustive Concordance of the Bible explains this love, "agapao," means unconditional love; love by choice and by an act of the will. The word denotes unconquerable, benevolence and undefeatable goodwill. Agapao will never seek anything but the highest good of mankind. It is the highest, noblest form of love. It sees something infinitely precious in its object. Agapao (verb) and *agape* (noun) are the words for God's eternal, unconditional love. It belongs exclusively to the heavenly community.

JOY

Joy given by the Spirit of God has the capability of lifting one's life above any circumstance or predicament. It is from the Spirit of God. The Spirit is its source. Joy is strength to every believer. "The joy of the Lord is my strength" according to Nehemiah 8:10. The outward expression of joy is rejoicing in God. It is not based on any outward condition but on the continual nurturing of the Holy Spirit inside the believer's heart. Jesus communicated to the people that joy is a relevant part of the Kingdom of God: "For the Kingdom of God is not eating and drinking, but righteousness and peace and joy in the Holy Spirit" (Romans 14:17).

PEACE

Jesus taught His followers as He prepared to leave the earth, "Peace I leave with you, My peace I give to you; not as the world gives do I give to you. Let not your heart be troubled, neither let it be afraid" (John 14:27). Peace carries with it the idea of rest, security, protection, and provision. The peace of the Holy Spirit is the calm assurance that God is always in the midst of life to comfort, protect, and deliver. It is the spiritual wellbeing of the Christian; it is the consciousness of right relationship with God.

PATIENCE

Patience or long-suffering speaks of steadfastness under provocation (Dictionary.com). Enduring without ill feelings or retaliatory actions is one description of patience. A tender heart and a spirit of humility endure the load of patience. In the word of God, patience is closely related to testing and trials. The believer is admonished to be patient when tried, for patience teaches one to draw strength from the eternal source— God. In order for the fruit of patience to manifest, sometimes a believer goes through chastening, discipline, affliction, and persecution (Paraphrased James 1:3). Therefore, each believer must employ long-suffering in order to endure until the fruit of patience "has her perfect work that you may be perfect and complete lacking nothing" (James 1:4).

KINDNESS

Kindness is a fruit that reaches outward toward others. It covers over harshness and reacts lovingly. The kind heart is a broken one (Paraphrased Psalm 51:17) that weeps for the poor and needy as well as for the rich. Kindness is goodness in action, sweetness of disposition, gentleness in dealing with others. The Holy Spirit progressively removes abrasive qualities from those under His control.

GOODNESS

Goodness refers to the character traits of an upright nobleman who is ruled by and aims at what is good. It represents the highest moral and ethical values (Paraphrased Psalm 112:5). In the language of scripture, it literally means "to be like God," for He alone is perfectly good. Goodness is doing good out of a good heart to please God.

FAITHFULNESS

Faithfulness is a characteristic of the inward man. The Spirit of God works "in" the believer that He might work "through" him. Faithfulness refers to fidelity or being dependable. Faithfulness is the dutifulness of a believer and the ability to stick to a task at hand. The ultimate reward for faithfulness is summed up in the last book of the Bible: "Be faithful until death, and I will give you the crown of life" (Revelations 2:10b).

GENTLENESS

Gentleness means mildness and respect in dealing with others (Dictionary.com). Those possessing the trait of gentleness give a soft answer that turns away wrath

(paraphrased Proverbs 15:1). Gentleness offers sympathy and care. It typifies quiet strength; it is love under discipline. Gentleness comes through having the sight of God. It illustrates that its host is at peace with power, never to abuse it. The gentle one has a humble heart.

SELF-CONTROL

Self-control or temperance comes from a Greek word which means strong, having mastery over one's thoughts and actions (*Webster's College Dictionary*). Self-control is the highest mark of nobility; it is kingly and regal. The sin of intemperance (lack of self-control) springs from two causes: physical appetite and mental habit. The Apostle Paul explained, "Those who live according to their sinful nature have their minds set on what that nature desires; but those who live according to the Spirit have their minds set on what the Spirit desires" (Romans 8:5). God progressively works in the believer to bring every aspect and level of him under the banner of self-control to save, preserve, and expand his life.

Developing the fruit of the Spirit is a must for all believers. God requires that the believer not only bear fruit, but bear "much" fruit for His glory (paraphrase John 15:8). This display reflects the perfect nature and character of God in the life of Christians. Without the fruit of the Spirit a Christian looks no different from one whose consciousness is focused on the world. The fruit of the Spirit encapsulates what the believer "looks like" or "becomes like" in his inner life. Initiated by the Holy Spirit, the process of developing the fruit of the Spirit begins the journey for newly born-again believers and veteran believers must fulfill the call to "be" like the heavenly Father from the inside out.

THE GIFTS OF THE HOLY SPIRIT

The Spirit of God is the source of power for the believer becoming part of God's Kingdom administration. As with Jesus, the third person of the trinity disperses His power to the believer for service to God. In 1 Corinthians 14:1 the Word of God proclaims: "Pursue love, and desire spiritual gifts." The power of the Holy Spirit authorizes the believer to exact heavenly forces on earth to establish the Kingdom of God. A king operates with power and authority. God gives this power and authority to His children that they might subdue the earth for His glory. This conscious working of the believer in the earthly realm also extends to the heavenly realm where God's rulership is evident.

To operate in the gifts of the Spirit by faith is to operate beyond the earthly dimension. "The nine gifts of the Spirit are the result of the Holy Spirit's infilling power" (Hagin, *The Holy Spirit and His Gifts* 27). When believers function at this level of Kingdom activity they operate in Kingdom consciousness.

The gifts that the Holy Spirit administered to Christians are similar to the fruit of the Spirit in that they are given by the Spirit. The gifts are imparted to each one "as the Spirit" sees fit. The source of all the gifts is the Spirit of God. Like the fruit of the Spirit, they are supernaturally imparted to the believer for the expanding of the church through the believer's witness (paraphrased 1 Corinthians 12:7). God demonstrates His love to the world through the believer's display of both the fruits and the gifts of the Spirit.

The gifts and the fruits of the Spirit are also similar in that

they all glorify the Father of Light. Because the gifts and the fruits of the Spirit cannot be bought or conjured up by the will of man God specifically desires the glory for the results of each used according to His proscribed method.

The gifts and the fruits of the Spirit are different, however, in distinct ways. All the fruits of the Spirit are given to each believer. Once the Holy Spirit takes up residence, He brings all nine into the heart and spirit of the believer (Hayford 1780). However, it is the responsibility of the believer to cultivate and develop them. Whereas, concerning the gifts, the Holy Spirit gives certain ones to certain people. No believer can choose which gift he receives; it is at the discretion of the Holy Spirit alone. The believer has the delight of discovering what gift the Holy Spirit has deposited within him, but the choice is a divine one.

The fruits of the Spirit are a divine reflection of God's character and nature. They begin to be evident immediately at salvation along with the Holy Spirit who then nurtures and develops them. On the other hand, the gifts of the Spirit can be deposited arbitrarily as they are received into the life of a believer.

The qualities of the fruits of the Spirit are about what God does; they are who He is. God does not merely love; He is Love. God does not just grant peace; He is Peace. The fruits of the Spirit have to do with God's character. They are the development of the nature of God within the Christian's spirit. On the other hand, the gifts of the Spirit have to

> *God does not merely love; He is Love. God does not just grant peace; He is Peace.*

do with empowerment for service to God (paraphrased Luke 24:49). These gifts from the Holy Spirit have to do with God's abilities demonstrated through mankind. While the power of the gifts is important, the character from the fruit is even more important because character protects the use of the power.

Power without character is dangerous. Therefore, balancing the two is a continuous challenge for most believers. Some

Power without character is dangerous.

theologians believe this is the reason Jesus spent so much time teaching the disciples how to think, how to live, and how to behave. Then when the Holy Spirit came with the poured-out power, enabling

them to display signs, wonders, and miracles, they had already developed the character to use the power rightly. Even after the disseminating of the supernatural power of the Holy Spirit, the Spirit of God continued to train and transform the disciples into what they were destined to become.

The Apostle Paul lists nine gifts of the Holy Spirit in the first letter to the Christians in Corinth around 56 A.D.:

> There are diversities of gifts, but the same Spirit. There are differences of ministries, but the same Lord. And there are diversities of activities, but it is the same God who works all in all. But the manifestation of the Spirit is given to each one for the profit of all: for to one is given the word of wisdom through the Spirit, to another the word of knowledge through the same Spirit, to another faith by the same Spirit, to another gifts of healings by the same Spirit, to another the working of miracles, to

another prophecy, to another discerning of spirits, to another different kinds of tongues, to another the interpretation of tongues (1Corinthians 12:4-10).

Paul recognized these gifts as supernatural abilities conferred on a believer by the Holy Spirit. They are spiritual manifestations of God's Spirit and exemplify evidence of the Holy Spirit's activity (Hayford 1736).

The gifts of the Spirit may also be categorized into three groups: utterance, power, and revelation. Word of wisdom, word of knowledge, and discerning between spirits form the group that "reveal" something—revelation gifts (Hagin 84). Prophecy, different kinds of tongues, and the interpretation of tongues "say" something—utterance gifts (Hagin 85). Faith, miracles, and healings are gifts that "do" something—power gifts (Hagin 84).

Concerning the gifts that reveal, the word of wisdom is utterance given by the Spirit that supernaturally discloses the mind, purpose, and way of God for a specific purpose. God has all wisdom and gives a fragment or a part of His wisdom for a situation at a particular time. "The word of wisdom always speaks to the future" (Hagin 102).

The word of knowledge is also a gift of supernatural revelation of information pertaining to a person or an event for a specific purpose. It usually has to do with an immediate need or issue in the present or past tense.

The discerning of spirits is another gift of the Spirit grouped in the revelation category. To discern means to discover, perceive, recognize, see, or distinguish, according to *Webster's College Dictionary*. To discern also mean to hear in the realm of the spiritual world—angels, demons, the voice of God.

"Therefore the gift of the discerning of spirits is to see and hear in the spiritual world" (Hagin 109).

The gifts of utterance all share the fact that they "say" something supernaturally. The gift of different kinds of tongues is the supernatural utterance gift in an unknown tongue or language. It is the gift of speaking supernaturally in a language not known to the speaker.

The gift of interpretation of tongues is the gift that renders a "transrational" message of the Spirit meaningful to others when spoken in public (Hayford 1737). It is not a literal translation of a language. However, it is the "showing forth" of what has been said when spoken in another language.

The gift of prophecy is a supernatural gift that edifies through revelatory disclosure. It prompts exhortation and comfort. "The Greek word for 'prophesy' means to speak for another" (Hagin 139). Divers kinds of tongues and the interpretation of tongues together equal the gift of prophecy.

In 1 Corinthians 14:3, Paul admonishes: "But he that prophesies speaks edification and exhortation and comfort to men." Therefore, the gift of prophecy is the supernatural ability to render divine insight that brings edification, exhortation, and comfort.

The gifts of the Spirit that entail the display of divine power "do" something. The gift of faith is a unique form of belief that goes beyond natural faith (common human faith) or saving faith (faith to believe in Jesus Christ as God's Son). There is a supernatural ability to trust and not doubt when this gift is active. The gift of faith is a supernatural ability to receive miracles. "The gift of faith does not work a miracle but passively receives a miracle" (Hagin 119).

On the other hand, "the gift of miracles does actively work a miracle" (Hagin 128). The gift of miracles is an act or function. Kenneth Hagin, in his book, *The Holy Spirit and His Gifts*, explains miracles as: "The supernatural intervention by God in the ordinary course of nature" (Hagin 126). The gift of miracles is a manifestation of power beyond the ordinary course of natural law. It is a divine enablement to do something that could not be done naturally.

The other "power" gift is healing. Gifts of healings are performed by the Holy Spirit supernaturally. This is expressed in the plural to suggest that as there are many types and kinds of diseases, God employs various methods of healings for the disease at hand—healings of many disorders. When the gifts of healings are on display: "it is usually administered by one person to another. God uses a vessel to channel the healing power through" (Hagin 135).

All the gifts of the Spirit are important and useful to the body of Christ. The Holy Spirit gives the gifts as He wills, distributing to each individual. While there are several gifts, they have a unity of purpose—to serve the body of Christ, enabling each member to take on the character of God and to use the power for the Kingdom of God. The authority and power a believer receives are for the service and the glory of the Father. They benefit one another, but are not for selfish use.

It is significant to consider that all the gifts of the Spirit work and operate by love. Without love, none of the heroic displays of power through men would prove advantageous. The Apostle Paul writes in 1 Corinthians 13 that even if one practices all of the gifts of the Spirit and has not love "it profits nothing." Love (manifested in all the fruits) is the benchmark of God's active transformation in the lives of His people. The fruit of the Spirit of Christ is the full harvest of righteousness.

Therefore, it is not the gifts that necessarily authenticate the presence of the Holy Spirit. The enemy of God can imitate a gift to deceive (paraphrased 2 Corinthians 11:14). But it is the mature fruits of the Spirit working in the inner heart of the believer that point toward the nature and character of the perfect God.

The purpose of the gifts of the Spirit of God is to serve

It is up to every believer to learn how to use the authority and power of the Holy Spirit's manifest presence in the correct way so as to deliver His works to the world and bring about changes commensurate with the standards of God's Kingdom.

the common good of mankind. Paul affirms that "the manifestation of the Spirit is given to each one for the profit of all" (1 Corinthians 12:7). The Holy Spirit is seen in the gifts and the fruits to benefit and profit all who would come into the Kingdom of God. It is up to every believer to learn how to use the authority and power of the Holy Spirit's manifest presence in the correct way so as to deliver His works to the world and bring about changes commensurate with the standards of God's Kingdom.

As witnessed and proven throughout the scriptures, the Holy Spirit plays an exceptional role in the translating of Kingdom of God consciousness to the believer in the realm of the earth. The Holy Spirit is God in the earth today, and He is the Power of the heavenly realm of God's Kingdom. The Holy Spirit was on the scene from the beginning; breathing life into Adam, the first man, forming the earth, performing signs to the nation of Israel, raising Jesus from the dead, bringing salvation to mankind, and transforming the life of man to reflect the life of God. The Holy Spirit executes the plan of God by empowering mankind with the eternal strength, gifts, and fruit of God's Spirit.

It is the Holy Spirit who teaches, coaches, administers, and imparts the mind of God and God's culture into the minds of men. The Holy Spirit, who is God, brings the entire heavenly sphere into the hearts of mankind in order to transform the world and the lives of humanity. He changes the inner culture of man from the direction of a darkened world into a consciousness filled with God's values, goals, and plans. The Holy Spirit brings to the world of man the transcendent Kingdom of God that goes beyond the unstable world of man's politics, unjust laws, unsettled institutions, and tottering religions.

The Holy Spirit is the bridge from the heavenly sphere to the earthly one. Through the Holy Spirit, the Word of God is enlightened to the believer that he may walk in the true Spirit of God's written epistles. The Holy Spirit is the Comforter, the Revealer of the truth. He is the Might and Strength of Heaven. The Holy Spirit carries out the plan for the believer as God so prescribed.

The Holy Spirit imparts God's life into the world of

The Holy Spirit brings to the world of man the transcendent Kingdom of God that goes beyond the unstable world of man's politics, unjust laws, unsettled institutions, and tottering religions.

mankind. The Holy Spirit is the change-agent in the minds and hearts of men and the guarantee that believers will possess their divine inheritance in heaven and on the earth. The Holy Spirit transports the vision, nature, mind-set, and values of God to the earth so that one day the new heaven and the new earth will appear, even in the transformation of the hearts of people. Change, then, will take place in all areas of life and in all peoples, languages, nationalities, and ethnicities.

Chapter

6

A Consciousness of Beliving and Executing

A Consciousness of Believing

The Kingdom of God rests on the consciousness of believing in the work of Christ on the cross. Therefore, having faith in God starts at having faith in the atoning death of Christ and his resurrection for eternal salvation. Hebrews 11:1 addresses the subject of faith: "Now faith is the substance of things hoped for, the evidence of things not seen." Faith is a living confidence and trust in God; in the experience of knowing God's presence as manifested in Jesus. Faith is seeing in the realm of the spiritual dimension and acting as though what is believed has already transpired. Faith perceives beyond current circumstances to what hope sees. "Without faith it is impossible to please God" (Hebrews 11:6).

Faith is having a consciousness about God and His power to bring His predestined plans to pass in the life of the believer and in the consummation of history. Confidence in God moves beyond the tendency to see the limitations of human weaknesses because it springs from what God has already accomplished through Christ. Without faith a believer would be paralyzed in the process of manifesting God's sovereign rule in the earth. He would not initiate walking in the Spirit of God nor exercise the power of God to bring healing and deliverance to nations.

Faith comes to the believer through hearing God's word (Romans 10:17). It is through the Word of God that the Holy Spirit awakens a response of faith in the hearts of men. The Word of God is the reliable source on which the believer rests his faith for salvation. The Holy Scripture is the word of eternal life. 1 Peter 1:23 verifies this: "having been born again, not of corruptible seed but incorruptible, through the word of God which lives and abides forever." The Kingdom of God is established on the Word of God. Therefore, the believer accesses all the dimensions of God's Kingdom through faith in His Word.

Kingdom of God consciousness begins with the individual believing in the work of Jesus on the cross for restoration of mankind's broken relationship with God. Mankind has to believe by faith (assurance of conviction or steadfast belief) what was done on the cross by Jesus and accept this work in his life to reap the resulting benefits. God-given faith helps an individual appropriate (know, understand, and apply) the work of the cross in his life and in every circumstance so that God may be seen.

Since the ultimate sacrifice of Jesus was to save the depraved human spirit, now the Holy Spirit can again live inside the human heart. Through faith, the spirit of man is

transformed, and at that point the Holy Spirit brings affirmation of the Kingdom of God to man's heart. He begins the journey of living out his divine destiny and heavenly calling, to have authority over the earth, to subdue it, and to have dominion over it, in the knowledge and power of the omnipotent God.

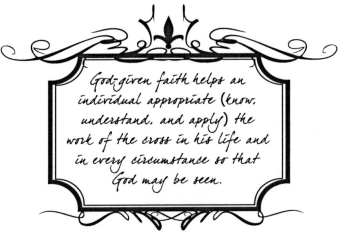

God-given faith helps an individual appropriate (know, understand, and apply) the work of the cross in his life and in every circumstance so that God may be seen.

THE PROCESS OF MIND RENEWAL

Once the spirit of man is born again (saved from eternal damnation), the process of mind renewal begins. This process involves a change or transformation in how man thinks, ultimately affecting how he lives his life on earth, and the choices he makes that should impact the world for Christ because his thinking, generally developed by social environments and family life, does not always conform to God's ways and thinking.

Jesus, in His discourse as recorded by Matthew, taught: "Come to Me all you who labor and are heavy laden, and I will give you rest. Take My yoke upon you and learn from Me, for I

am gentle and lowly in heart, and you will find rest for your souls" (Matthew 11:28-29). Jesus explained that there should be a "learning" of Him. One has to be reeducated to the ways of God and the understanding of His Kingdom culture. This process takes place through searching the scripture, a devotional spiritual life of prayer and fasting, and implementing the laws of God in daily life. The process inevitably involves revision of the way a person sees himself in relationship to God. A new believer's perspective changes as his mind is transformed by the Holy Spirit and the Word of God.

The soul of man, which houses his mind, goes through a transformative process to eliminate malignancies that operate against the rule of God (including imaginations, past hurts, unforgiveness, and any other entity opposing the truth of God). According to *Strong's Exhaustive Concordance of the Bible*, the mind of man is "the seat of reflective consciousness, comprising the faculties of perception and understanding and those of feeling, judging, and determining; it is the seat of understanding" (Strong 173). Because the mind occupies a dominant role in the soul realm, the terms are often used interchangeably. The mind dictates thoughts and actions, and thoughts and actions make up who a person truly is. Proverbs 23:7 indicates: "For as he [man] thinks in heart, so is he." Therefore, man's being encompasses what he thinks and what he does (actions).

Consequently, Jesus encouraged mankind to change his thinking in order to embrace and integrate the culture of God's Kingdom within his actions. There is an unavoidable stretching of man's worldly consciousness to become centered on God's Kingdom awareness. This process has to take place in order for man to have a heightened awareness of God's sphere of rulership.

The Apostle Paul explains the believer's service to God in surrendering to this process: "And do not be conformed to this world, but be transformed by the renewing of your mind, that you may prove what is that good and acceptable and perfect will of God" (Romans 12:2). Through the guidance of the Holy Spirit this formation takes place to supplant the old way (the inherited way) of thinking.

For example, in ancient Judaic tradition it was taught: "An eye for an eye, a tooth for a tooth." Whatever wrong was committed against you, you had the right to do the same to the perpetrator. However, when Jesus began to teach about the Kingdom of God he instructed the people to love not only those who love them, but also their enemies. It was taught in the Law of Moses not to commit adultery (sexual misconduct). But through Jesus' teaching of the Kingdom of God the people were given a new awareness that to look at a person with a heart of lust was sinful in God's view.

The transformation in the mind has to be reflective of the change that has taken place in the heart and spirit of man. The mind plays a pivotal role in the development of the believer in the Kingdom of God. It was advised through the teachings of the Apostle Paul that the believer should allow the same "mind" that was in Christ to be in him also (paraphrased Philippians 2:5). Christ had a mind or an attitude centered and focused on the plans of His Father. Everything that He did was influenced by the will of His Father. This same attitude and disposition are what any believer should strive toward in the Christian life.

The mind dictates the difference between a life born anew (born of the Spirit of God) and a life born with effective power to possess and acquire the results of living in God's Kingdom. The born-again life places a believer in the realm of positional inheritance of God (paraphrased Ephesians 1:3). However, a life with a changed and transformed mind experiences the inheritance and the promises of God. The difference between knowing the promises of God and possessing the promises of God is a transformed mind.

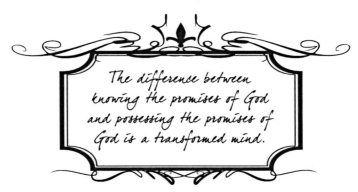

> The difference between knowing the promises of God and possessing the promises of God is a transformed mind.

Many Christians (believers of Christ Jesus) live a defeated life (subject to the dictates of the world of fallen mankind) even though they have access to the promises and blessings of God. This is because the minds of many believers still operate in the sphere of the natural world and not the realm of the spiritual world of God. The laws and statues of God, which include the teachings of Christ and the Apostles, are spiritual and not physical or based in logic. Therefore, the believer has to live and operate according to the dictates of the spiritual realm in order to manifest God's victory in his daily life and circumstances.

Believers live simultaneously in both the earthly and spiritual dimensions. This is the matrix in which a believer has

to process. Once the mind of God is revealed to a person's spirit by the Holy Spirit the believer begins to be acclimated to the consciousness of God in his thought life.

Christians should always be conscious of the spiritual realm because the things of God can only be discerned spiritually (paraphrased 1 Corinthians 2:14). Believers whose spirits have been infused with and recreated by the Holy Spirit can discern and understand the spiritual realm and walk in its mandates. In this dimension, the believer becomes familiar with the mind of God and the ways of God so that the divine plans for humanity may manifest in the earth. The problem of the Christian not yet engaged to live in the spiritual realm is his lack of power over the struggles that inundate the natural life. According to author Lloyd Ogilvie in his book, The *Magnificent Vision*, this type of believer can become "befuddled and even immobilized by the perplexity of human nature. [The struggling Christian can become] defeated over this own nature, thoughts, fantasies, actions, and reactions" (Ogilvie 21). The life in Christ has to continually progress in its ultimate fulfillment, being "changed into the image of Jesus Christ." Eternal life with Christ is settled, but then the believer progresses toward the understanding that eternal life also means a life of abundance here on earth. In John's gospel, Jesus makes this progression very clear: "I have come that they may have life, and that they may have it more abundantly" (John 10:10). The word "abundant" in the Greek (perissos) means "superabundance, excessive, overflowing, surplus, over and above, more than enough, profuse, extraordinary, above the ordinary, more than sufficient" (Strong 199).

Life in Christ is perpetual and continual throughout all

eternity. However, the "more abundant" life in Christ is given as a polarizing effect against the enemy of God, Satan. The first part of the scripture in John 10:10 notes that the enemy or the thief comes to kill, steal, and destroy the human life (paraphrased). Nonetheless, Christ came to do exactly the opposite of what was performed in the garden with Adam and Eve's submission to Satan's deception. Christ gave Himself to mankind. With Christ comes all the fullness of God: goodness, life, healing, and prosperity of spirit, soul, and body.

Christ gave life in abundance, not mere existence. Believing in this full life of Christ is the first step toward renewing the mind in the realm of Kingdom reality and experiencing God's highest desires for His people.

God does not only desire that His people be born again in spirit, but also that His people have abundant life in every area of their earthly life. The Apostle John announced: "Beloved, I pray that you may prosper in all things and be in health, just as your souls prosper" (3 John 1:2). Pastor and author Jack Hayford comments in the article "Prosperity Is a Result" in the *Spirit Filled Life Bible*:

> Prosperity is a result of the quality of life, commitment, dedication, and action that is in line with God's Word. Prosperity is an on-going, progressing state of success and well-being. It is intended for every area of our lives: the spiritual, the physical, and emotional, and the material (Hayford 1941).

God's prosperity in life through Christ is synonymous with having the mind renewed in the truth of God, and this truth should permeate the thoughts and actions of the believer. The believer's Kingdom perspective, thoughts, and actions should distinguish him from any other person in the world because he thinks like God, operating in the earthly sphere with a heavenly mindset.

The mind holds a powerful position in the human life because the thought processes of man will influence his actions.

A person's pattern of thought is a sound indicator of what the outcome of his situations will be. Thinking is the mind's rehearsal of what to say and what to do. Thoughts have the ability to manifest the world around a person. Thought patterns—which include concepts, ideas, mental understanding, awareness, notions, and images—frame the mental direction and the words spoken by the thinker. Therefore, thoughts and words produce a world with simultaneous effect.

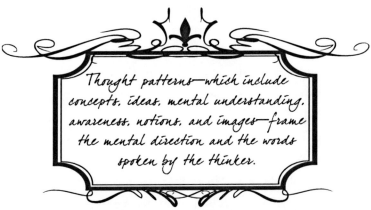

Thought patterns—which include concepts, ideas, mental understanding, awareness, notions, and images—frame the mental direction and the words spoken by the thinker.

Consequently, Proverbs 23:7 is a warning to all people that whatever they think upon becomes a pattern that governs their lives. In addition: "Death and life are in the power of the tongue" (Proverbs 18:21). The thoughts and words coming from the heart of man have the capacity to affect his physical and spiritual life. This is why having the mind of Christ (where

thoughts and words are formed in God consciousness) produces harmony with God's will.

Because mankind has the full life of Christ dwelling within him, he also has creative potential similar to God's (paraphrased Colossians 1:27). If God spoke the worlds into existence then whatever man speaks and meditates on will also manifest into existence. The ideas of a man produce his words and the words of man eventually produce his environment.

Attitudes of a Godly Mind

There are attitudes of the mind that every believer must develop in order to advance his spiritual development. As stated by *Webster's College Dictionary*, an attitude is "a manner, disposition, feeling, or position with regard to a person or thing; a tendency or orientation, especially of the mind; a posture." An attitude of the mind is its expressive position, posture, or orientation. An attitude is also a habitual or characteristic mental perception. The believer should contend for the mental attitudes that Christ possessed.

In Matthew 26:39, the text describes Christ's obedience to His Father: "He went a little further and fell on His face and prayed saying, oh my Father, if it is possible let this cup pass from Me; nevertheless, not as I will, but as you will." Christ was obedient to His Father beyond His own comfort. He knew the reason He had come to the earth; to serve all mankind. Jesus is noted as providing the highest standard of service when He said: "Just as the Son of Man did not come to be served but to serve and to give His life as a ransom for many" (Matthew 20:28). He humbled Himself to death on a cross to accomplish God's will.

Christ also employed self-discipline to aid in staying true to

His focus of pleasing God. The prophet Isaiah wrote about the discipline of Christ: "He was oppressed and He was afflicted, yet He opened not His mouth; He was led as a lamb to the slaughter and as a sheep before its shearers is silent, so He opened not His mouth" (Isaiah 53:7).

OBEDIENCE

The mental attitude of obedience is of optimal importance to any believer as he progresses to know God and forges forward in God's predetermined will for his life. Obedience is not only an attitude of the heart; it is a discipline of the mind that translates into the "action" of obeying. The Word of God states in Isaiah 1:19: "If you are willing and obedient, you shall eat the good of the land." Willingness is a matter of the heart; however, to accomplish the action is a mental resolve, a conscious decision executed. God desires not just the act of obedience, but a heart of submission because one can accomplish the directive without submitting to the one initiating the directive. Therefore the mere act of obeying is inadequate. God desires a heart of submission. Regarding the restoration of the nation of Israel during the time of the prophet Ezekiel, God announced:

> Then I will give them one heart, and I will put a new spirit within them, and take the stony heart out of their flesh, and give them a heart of flesh, that they may walk in My statutes and keep my judgments and do them; and they shall be My people, and I will be their God (Ezekiel 11:19-20).

Obedience hinges on a heart of submission, an attitude of surrendering to the rule of God. In summation, obedience from the heart is an attitude of the mind that God prizes.

SERVANTHOOD

Jesus is the ultimate example to the believer and to the world of how one should conduct a life submitted to God and His authority. In Matthew 20:28, Jesus explains that His role as the Son of Man was not to be served but to serve others. Servanthood denotes a disposition of lowliness in how one places others' needs and wants before his own. The meaning of a servant, according to *Strong's Exhaustive Concordance of the Bible*, is "doulos" in the Greek (Strong 72). This word translated is a "bond man" or a slave; one who is in "permanent relation of servitude to another as his will is completely subjected to the will of another" (Strong 72). With the word "servant" the focus is not on what work is performed, but on the relationship to the master. "The word slave, originally the lowest term on the scale of servitude, came also to mean one who gives himself up for the will of another" (Strong 72).

Selfless servanthood is the mark of a mind surrendered in its attitude toward God and His Word (Riley 8). Servants pursue the good of their masters as they seek to please them.

So it is with a believer who has the mind of Christ. His will is to be aligned with serving God by serving the people God has assigned him to aid. A believer with a servant's heart executes service willingly and with pleasure. He puts his own desires last in order to care for the needs of others. A true servant does this out of the relationship he has with his master, not for money or to be praised by others.

The mother of James and John, two of Jesus' original disciples, came to Him and asked if her two sons could sit in places of honor in His coming Kingdom (paraphrased Matthew

20:20-21). Jesus' response was summed up in His explanation regarding serving mankind: "...Whoever desires to become great among you, let him be your servant. Whoever desires to be first among you, let him be your slave" (Matthew 20:26-27).

The attitude of the believer's mind, according to Jesus' teaching to the disciples, was that "true greatness is measured in terms of service" (Hayford 1444). Therefore Jesus personified servanthood and provided the highest standard of service in His atoning death.

Humility

Humility comes from a word that means "absolute dependence, of possessing nothing and receiving all things from God" (Strong 247). Humility denotes understanding the lowliness of everything created, including human beings. It is associated with exalting God, the Creator. The attitude of humility of mind stamps out pride and haughtiness; it is the direct opposite.

Pride raises itself up against God's directives and is evidence of an impending downfall of the one who allows it to overtake him. Proverbs 16:18 states: "Pride goes before destruction and a haughty spirit before a fall." The Apostle Paul warned of the calamity that accompanies pride of an immature leader. To avoid it requires developing more in the faith and becoming more experientially mature. The Apostle explains the requirements of an overseer to his protégé, Pastor Timothy: "[He should] not be a novice lest being puffed up with pride he fall into the same condemnation as the devil" (1 Timothy 3:6).

Concurrently, humility can indicate abasing or

mortification. According to *Webster's College Dictionary*, humility is to abase oneself in thought and actions so as to be under or submitted to another. It describes a person who is "devoid of all arrogance and self-exaltation; willingly submitted to God and His will" (Hayford 1439). The Apostle Peter, in his letter to various churches in Asia Minor during the suffering of rejection in the world because of their obedience to Christ, addressed the Christians: "Therefore humble yourselves under the mighty hand of God, that He may exalt you in due time" (1 Peter 5:6). In relationships of any kind the mind of the believer should grasp the fundamentals of humility and lowliness so that God Himself will be the One to approve, promote, commend, and exalt.

DISCIPLINE

Discipline is defined as a type of training. This training is to produce actions in accordance with God's rules. *Webster's College Dictionary* instructs that discipline is "activity, exercise, or regimen that develops or improves a skill; it is the correction of a behavior. It is to bring to a state of order and obedience by training and control." God trains His people in the conduct and actions of Kingdom heirs, and He disciplines those who belong to Him.

Hebrews 12 states that God disciplines His children like a father would discipline his offspring for their training and correction. In this passage, God is dealing with His children as sons (paraphrased Hebrews 12:6-8). Thus, if God does not discipline a person, then that one does not belong to God. Hebrews 12:8 teaches: "But if you are without chastening of which all have become partakers, then you are illegitimate and not sons." In God's view, undisciplined children are relegated to "illegitimate" status.

Discipline is not only initiated by God, but the believer is to be proactive in the development of discipline in his own spiritual life.

Discipline is not only initiated by God, but the believer is to be proactive in the development of discipline in his own spiritual life. Christians learn to refuse any work of the flesh (carnal nature) and any solicitation from Satan. The Apostle Paul listed the works of the flesh in Galatians 5:18-21:

> Now the works of the flesh are evident, which are: adultery, Fornication, uncleanness, lewdness, idolatry, sorcery, hatred, contentions, jealousies, outbursts of wrath, selfish ambitions, dissentions, heresies, envy, murders, drunkenness, revelries, and the like; of which I tell you beforehand, just as I told you in time past, that those who practice such things will not inherit the kingdom of God.

Followers of Christ, with a disciplined attitude and mindset, continuously train themselves in right living, hence choosing to obey God. In addition, they are instructed to yield to God while resisting the devil in his tactical threats against God's people. James 4:7 instructs: "Therefore submit to God, resist the devil and he will flee from you."

Yielding to God in everything is a discipline that every believer must develop in order to have a victorious life in Christ. It takes training to be victoriously successful in defeating every attack that the devil might hurl at the mind, the circumstances, and the life of a believer. Although sometimes painful, being self-controlled in thoughts, actions, and decisions keeps the believer protected in the will of God until he is fully developed and matured. Outside God's will is a dangerous place for a believer since it can leave him unprotected. God's determined will is a safe covering for all Disciples of Christ. For every believer, staying under this fortified covering requires self-control and adherence to God's rulership.

Godly attitudes of the mind are part of the transformative process to which every believer must adhere. Christians should not conform to the thoughts and mental patterns of this worldly age and godless system. They are encouraged to be changed in the attitudes of their minds to reflect the thoughts and attitudes of Christ. It is important that those who believe in Christ become committed to the ideals of the Kingdom of God. Believers learn to put their total confidence in Christ because He is "the author and finisher of the faith."

WHOLENESS AND COMPLETION

God corrects and disciplines, renews and changes the mindset and personality of the believer to conform to His purpose and plan. God is determined to make the believer "complete" and whole in his quest for divine purpose and destiny. James 1:4 declares: "But let patience have its perfect work that you may be perfect and complete, lacking nothing."

God desires to heal and mend every broken aspect of the believer's life through processing, discipline, and healing. The Apostle Paul asked the question to the divided Christians in Corinth in 56 A.D.: "Is Christ divided?" (1 Corinthians 1:13).

The obvious answer is that Christ is not divided, and every believer should introspectively assure himself of no divisions in relationship between himself and other believers. Jesus, in His earthly ministry, was not fragmented, broken, or divided. He was whole and unbroken with no division.

This state of wholeness is the completed state of man when he is mature and complete, lacking nothing (James 1:4). In comforting the Thessalonian Christians, Paul assured them through his prayer: "Now may the God of peace Himself sanctify you completely; and may your whole spirit, soul, and body be preserved blameless at the coming of our Lord Jesus Christ" (1 Thessalonians 5:23). The Holy Spirit's constant instructions to the believer signify that the process of development is yet underway. God is mending and bringing wholeness of the personality of the believer into view.

The Apostle Paul argued with the Corinthians concerning their obvious carnality (sign of an immature believer). Paul vehemently pointing out that divisions among them occurred because of strife and envy, denoting that the Corinthians were carnal and not spiritual: "For you are still carnal. For where there are envy, strife, and divisions among you, are you not carnal and behaving like mere men?" (1Corinthians 3:3).

There are all types of brokenness in believers. However, through the powerful acts of God's healing restoration, He displays His unconditional love. By affirming and reshaping the personality of man God strengthens who the believer truly is while maintaining the uniqueness He has placed within each individual. The wholeness that God brings indicates who the believer truly is underneath the veneers of worldly values, self-defeating attitudes, and ungodly actions he demonstrates.

During times of prayer and devotion, God begins to tenderly expose areas of the believer's life that need to be reshaped and remolded to be more like Him:

> God reforms anything that distorts or hinders the believer's becoming all that God meant him to be. God frees the believer with new values, priorities, attitudes, and goals which begin to surface in the personality. Human nature can be changed (Ogilvie 155-156).

The believer goes through a refining process where God begins to remove those components that do not comply with His will. Revelations 3:18-19 Amplified, states:

> Therefore I counsel you to purchase from Me gold refined and tested by fire that you may be truly wealthy, and white clothes to cloth you and keep the shame of your nudity from being seen, and salve to put on your eyes that you may see. Those that I dearly and tenderly love, I tell their faults and convict and convince and reprove and chasten [I discipline and instruct them]. So be enthusiastic and in earnest and burning with zeal and repent [changing your mind and attitude].

Wholeness is the desire of God for His people that they might demonstrate to the world His Kingdom ideal of unconditional love. God works in the believer that He may work through the believer so the world might have a reference

to model after. "Resting in the place of completion will free [the believer] from the pressure of wanting to be someone else" (Long 163).

Experiencing wholeness through Jesus Christ is God's invitation to the believer to undergo a radical transformation of the entire human existence. As one is rooted in the word of God and grows into maturity he is free to be his true self; the image that God intended. This radical change and transformation takes place inside the spirit and soul

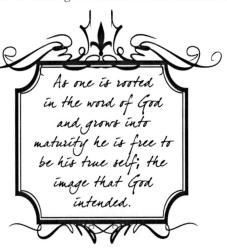

As one is rooted in the word of God and grows into maturity he is free to be his true self; the image that God intended.

of man because "everything that was manifested in the character of Jesus is reproducible in [the believer]" (Ogilvie 160). As the believer crucifies the flesh (carnal desires and actions), develops in spiritual maturity, exhibits the fruit of the Spirit (love, joy, peace, longsuffering, kindness, goodness, faithfulness, gentleness and self-control), and grows in his relationship with God and His Word, he can be entrusted with becoming a channel through whom the Kingdom of God is promulgated and illustrated to the world.

A CONSCIOUSNESS OF EXECUTING

Wholeness in the spirit, soul, and body of human beings positions them to carry out the Kingdom of God mandate.

God's Kingdom comes into the believer after he is born again by the Spirit. As a result, God uses the believer in the earthly realm as a vessel through which the Kingdom flows into the world. Matthew 6:10 explains: "Your kingdom come, Your will be done on earth as it is in heaven." God works through His sons and daughters on the earth.

To be a channel for the Kingdom of God, divine processing has to take place for the believer to be able to wield the power, love, and authority of God the way God intended.

The authority of God is God's power delegated or entrusted to His heirs. Ephesians 2:6 affirms the authority that the believer has in Christ: "And has raised us up together, and made us sit together in the heavenly places in Christ Jesus." Believers share in the authority of Christ as they are developed in Him. After the processing of man's spirit and soul (mind) there is a revealing of man as a son of God in the earth. Romans 8:19 elucidates: "For the earnest expectation of the creation eagerly waits for the revealing of the sons of God."

To reveal means to uncover, to exhibit, to manifest to the awareness of; to make known and to disclose; to lay open to view. According to *Strong's Exhaustive Concordance of the Bible*, the word "reveal" means "something that is presented to the mind directly, or the mind of God to the church" (Strong 36). God desires to disclose to the world those who are truly His children. God wants the earth and all the heavenly hosts to see those through which He will work His power.

In the book of Ephesians, the Apostle Paul writes concerning God's vast wisdom in His plan that included a visible defeat of the powers of Satan by the church: "To the intent that now the manifold wisdom of God might be made known by the church to the principalities and powers in the heavenly places" (Ephesians 3:10). These sons of God are the ones who will possess the territory that had been surrendered to Satan. Jesus made this possible through His atoning death; with the help of the Holy Spirit, the believer makes this acquisition a real experience in the earthly realm.

God does this to show His multi-various wisdom through His church, His believers, and to all the earthly and heavenly realms. The Apostle Paul explains God's purpose for the role of the church through Christ:

And to make all see what is the fellowship of the mystery, which from the beginning of the ages has been hidden in God who created all things through Jesus Christ to the intent that now the manifold wisdom of God might be made known by the church to the principalities and powers in the heavenly places according to the eternal purpose which He accomplished in Christ Jesus our Lord (Ephesians 9-11).

Believers are this channel of the expressed and revealed will of God to "go in and possess" what God has made available to them. God requires that all the initial territory given to Adam be retrieved. "Every place that the sole of your foot will tread upon I have given you" (Joshua 1:3). God, at this point in a believer's life, has invested tremendous time, power, deliverance, instruction, transformative work, and guidance. Therefore, God does this that His believers would think, act, and be like He is, thus imposing God's rule in the earth. God sets His people in the conscious frame to fight and win. As He told David when he inquired for directions in fighting the Amalekites: "Pursue, for you shall surely overtake them and without fail recover all" (1 Samuel 30:8).

When the fight against the instruments of Satan's diabolical powers results in miraculous victory for the people of God, it is evident that God is revealing His glory (supernatural grace and power) through His believers. Winning back territory—not only land and material entities, but also peace, joy, health, prosperity, and the souls of men— are all part of God's plan to execute His Kingdom program. As Pastor and Bishop Eddie Long unravels in his book, *Taking Over*: "The church of the living God is ordained and anointed to go into enemy territory, snatch people out of darkness, and bring them into the marvelous light...God is looking for soldiers" (Long 10).

Through the power of Christ, the believer is the extension of God in the earth to execute God's original plan that His sons and daughters reign in the earth as He reigns in heaven. Jesus declared the power that was bestowed upon His disciples as with all believers: "Behold, I give you the authority to trample on serpents and scorpions and over all the power of the enemy, and nothing shall by any means hurt you" (Luke 10:19).

THE LAW OF DOMINION

God desires that man regain dominion over the earth that Adam had been given before he fell into disobedience. In Genesis 1:26 and 28, God publicly declared:

Let Us make man in Our image, according to Our likeness; let them have dominion over the fish of the sea, over the birds of the air, and over the cattle, over all the earth and over every creeping thing that creeps on the earth...Then God blessed them, and God said to them, be fruitful and multiply; fill the earth and subdue it; have dominion over the fish of the sea, over the birds of the air, and over every living thing that moves on the earth).

It is clear that God gave authority over the earth to mankind to rule and have dominion. Dominion means "to prevail, to reign, to rule, to tread down, to subdue" (Strong 258). God decided on dominion for the destiny of mankind, and He has not changed His plan. "Dominion is a Kingdom law" (Robertson 199). Throughout the scripture, God executed His strategy of redemption through empowering man to defeat

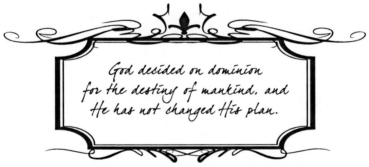

God decided on dominion for the destiny of mankind, and He has not changed His plan.

all enemies (including all who would stop mankind from pursuing the will of God, including, especially, Satan). "God has gone through great lengths to make this possible, sending his own Son as the second Adam to restore what was lost in Eden" (Robertson 199).

When God brought all the creatures of the earth to Adam to see what he would name them, whatever he called them that was their name (Genesis 2:19). In this depiction of Adam's role in the earth, he exercised authority under God's sovereignty over everything on the earth. Adam was God's steward and agent in the earthly sphere. The word dominion in the Greek has two derivative words. The first is: "radah, which means to rule over or tread down, to prostrate or spread out" (Strong 258). The visual representation is that everywhere man would go creation would prostrate itself at his feet willingly. The second is: "kabash" translated "subdue." This word is the picture of trampling under foot as in "separating the good from the evil by force" (Robertson 200). With both words combined, God gave man sweeping authority to rule over the entire earth—that which willingly submits to his government (radah) and that which is to submit by force (kabash), the rebellious and the untamed.

God's fundamental aim was to give earthly reign and governmental authority to those who would submit to His rule and sovereignty. When man can assert God's dominion over himself, he accordingly has the capacity to execute God's dominion over every aspect of the earthly realm. If man refuses

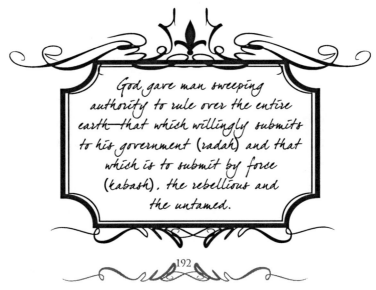

God gave man sweeping authority to rule over the entire earth—that which willingly submits to his government (radah) and that which is to submit by force (kabash), the rebellious and the untamed.

to exercise authority over the earth and over Satan's kingdom then man himself becomes the one subdued. This is the reason believers must exercise dominion in their daily lives.

God has placed mankind in the position of power recaptured by Christ. Believers can yet experience a defeated life when they refuse to implement God's governmental authority in the earth. This is the process whereby everything on earth will be freed from the cycle of decay, bondage, corruption, and death. In the Apostle Paul's epistle to the Roman church in 56 A.D., he plainly contended:

> For the earnest expectation of the creation eagerly waits for the revealing of the sons of God. For the creation was subjected to futility, not willingly, but because of Him who subjected it in hope; because the creation itself also will be delivered from the bondage of corruption into the glorious liberty of the children of God. For we know that the whole creation groans and labors with birth pains together until now (Romans 8:18-22).

THE RESULTS

The Kingdom of God requires the believer to be transformed from a consciousness of the world to an awareness of the Kingdom of Light. This is the continual process to which Christians must be unreservedly dedicated. Through soul processing and mind transformation, God takes away from the human dimension what does not glorify or reflect His culture. In addition, He replaces the thought patterns and actions unlike His character with those corresponding to His divine nature and places them in the mindset of His people. God initiates this sacred operation through the atoning death of Christ, the power of Holy Spirit, and His Word. Consequently, the execution of dominion over Satan and the earth in general takes place through a processed and transformed life.

Dominion is the mandate of God for mankind in the earth. Without authority and dominion, mankind cannot carry out God's directive of subduing the earth and bringing it under the control and alignment of God's sovereign will. Kingdom of God consciousness denotes the rule of God in the earth executed through the power of the Holy Spirit in the transformed life of believers in Jesus Christ.

CONCLUSION

The Kingdom of God is a Kingdom of consciousness, an awareness of God's sovereignty in the heavenly realm as well as the earthly realm. This responsiveness to God's rulership assists the believer in operating in the sphere where God's authority extends to the earthly realm. As expressed in Matthew 6:10: "Your Kingdom come. Your will be done on earth as it is in heaven." God's initial intent was to create mankind to be like Him as man administered authority in the earth like God executes rulership in heaven. God chose to position mankind as His extension of the divine Kingdom on earth to rule and have dominion.

With the fall of Adam and Eve, mankind lost dominion and surrendered it to Satan who became man's enemy as he was already God's enemy. Because of the sin of man through separation from God, various consciousnesses came into the world through mankind's constructions such as the religious, economic, political, military, education, healthcare, and legal systems. In addition, these competing consciousnesses continue to polarize man from the awareness of God's sphere of influence. Now mankind must struggle to regain an understanding of God's nature and methodology.

In God's redemptive plan, He provided the atoning death of Jesus Christ, which would reconcile mankind back to God. Through this reconciliation process, God imparted the Holy Spirit into the hearts of man, which involved the mind of God flowing back to the consciousness of the believer as well as a reinstitution of man's ability to implement God's will through earthly dominion. In addition, man was rendered Godly authority and power on earth. Therefore, mankind has the privilege of abiding in the sphere of Kingdom awareness where God reigns, where mankind is subjected to God's government, and where the whole earth participates in rendering glory to God.

BIBLIOGRAPHY

- Adler, Mortimer J. *The Common Sense of Politics*. New York: Fordham University Press, 1996.

- *American Journal of Public Health*. Mary Northridge. ed. American Public Health Association.

- Baldwin, Lewis. *The Boundaries of Law, Politics and Religion*. Notre Dame: Notre Dame University Press, 1998.

- Barnhart, Fred D. "The Collapse of Enron." Law and technology resources for legal professionals. 15 Aug 2002. http://www.llrx.com/features/enron.htm#enron

- "Brown v. Board of Education." Brown Foundation for Educational Equality, Excellence and Research. 11 April 2004. <http://www.brownvboard.org/summary/index.php>.

- Brown, Lester. *State of the World*. New York: WW Norton & Company, 1992.

- "Bureaucracy." *The American Heritage® Dictionary of the English Language, Fourth Edition*. Houghton Mifflin Company, 2004. 27 Jun. 2009. <Dictionary.com http://dictionary.reference.com/browse/bureaucracy>.

- Bureau of Labor Statistics, U.S. Department of Labor, *Career Guide to Industries, 2008-09 Edition*, Health Care, on the Internet at http://www.bls.gov/oco/cg/cgs035. 08 Aug 2009.

- Chadwick, Henry. *The Early Church*. London: Penguin Group, 1993.

- Charles, Audrey E. *Hidden In Plain Sight*. Lithonia: New Revelations Publishers, 2005.

- Clarke, Paul. *Dictionary of Ethics, Theology and Society*. London: Rutledge, 1996.

- Costello, Robert B., Ed. *Random House Webster's College Dictionary*. New York: Random House, 1991.

- "Democracy." Democracy Building. 18 Aug 2009. http://www.democracy-building.info/definition-democracy.html.

- Denemark, Robert. *World System History*. New York: Routledge, Taylor and Francis Group, 2000.

- Dictionary. Com Website. 08 Aug 2009. http://dictionary.reference.com/.

- Eitzen, Stanley, and Maxine Baca-Zinn. *In Conflict and Order*, 9th Edition. Boston: Allyn and Bacon, 2001.

- Elson, Henry William. *History of the United States of America*. Trans. Kathy Leigh. New York: The MacMillan Company, 1904.

- "Enron Scandal At-A-Glance." BBC News World Edition. 22 Aug 2002.

- Fowler, Michael. "Isaac Newton." University of Virginia, Physics Department. 08 Aug 2009. <http://galileoandeinstein.physics.virginia.edu/lectures/newton.html>.

BIBLIOGRAPHY

- Friedman, Benjamin. *The Moral Consequences of Economic Growth.* New York: Knopf, 2005.

- Gaudstad, Edwin. *Church and State in America.* New York: Oxford Press, 1998.

- "Genetics and Heredity." Volume 3. Aug 2009. *The Genetics Society Website.* 16 Aug 2009. http://www.nature.com/hdy/index.html.

- Gottwald, Norman K. *The Hebrew Bible: A Socio-Literary Introduction.* Philadelphia: Fortress Press, 1985.

- Graham, Billy. *The Holy Spirit: Activating God's Power in Your Life.* Waco: Word Books, 1978.

- Grimm, Carl. *Greek-English Lexicon of the New Testament.* Corrected ed. New York: American Book Company, 1977.

- Gutek, Gerald. "The History of Education." Loyola University Department of Education 2009. Chicago IL. 04 Aug 2009. < http://Encarta.msn.com/text/History_of_education.html>.

- Hagin, Kenneth E. *Bible Faith Study Course.* Tulsa: Faith Library Publications, 1991.

- Hagin, Kenneth E. *The Holy Spirit and His Gifts.* Tulsa: Faith Library Publications, 1991.

- Hagin, Kenneth E. *The Believer's Authority.* Second Edition. Tulsa: Faith Library Publications, 1986.

- Halsall, Paul. "Development of a World Economic System." New York: Academic Press, 1997. http://www.fordham.edu/halsall/mod/wallerstein.html

- Harrison, E. F. *Baker's Dictionary of Theology*. Grand Rapids, MI: Zondervan, 1975.

- Hayford, Jack W. *People Of The Spirit*. Nashville: Thomas Nelson Publisher, 1994.

- Hayford, Jack W., ed. *Spirit Filled Life Bible*, New King James Version. Nashville: Thomas Nelson Publisher, 1991.

- "Health Care Statistics." Prevent Disease Website. 18 Aug 2009. http://preventdisease.com/worksite_wellness/health_stats.html.

- Henry, Matthew. *Concise Commentary On The Bible*. Nashville: Thomas Nelson Publisher, 1997.

- Hermann, Strack. *Introduction to the Talmud and Midrash*. Jewish Publication Society, 1945.

- Hickman, Kennedy. "Leading At Sea." The New York Times Company, 2009. http://militaryhistory.about.com/

- Horton, Stanley. *What the Bible Says About the Holy Spirit*. Springfield: Gospel Publishing House, 1976.

- "International Trade": *A Source of King Solomon's Wealth*. United States and Britain In Bible Prophecy. http://www.ucg.org/booklets/US/solomonswealth.asp

- "Jihad." *Wikipedia, The Free Encyclopedia*. 28 Jun 2009, 16:21 UTC. 28 Jun 2009

<http://en.wikipedia.org/w/index.php?title=Jihad&oldid=299139796>.

- "Judaism." Just the Facts on Religion Website. 08 Aug 2009. <http://www.religionfacts.com/Judaism/>.

- Kelly, J. N. D. *Early Christian Doctrines.* New York: HarperSanFrancisco, 1960.

- Kim, Jaegwon. *Philosophy of the Mind.* Boulder, CO: Westview Press, 2005.

- Kjeilen, Tore. "The Armenian Orthodox Church." 1996. 08 Aug 2009. <http://i-cias.com/e.o/arm_orth.htm>.

- Laymon, Charles M., ed. *The Interpreter's One-Volume Commentary On The Bible.* Nashville: Abington Press, 1991.

- Long, Eddie. *Taking Over, Seizing Your City for God in the New Millennium.* Lake Mary: Charisma House, 1999.

- Long, Eddie. *The Real Kingdom* (Sermon). New Birth Baptist Church. 2009.

- MacMullen, Ramsey. *Corruption and the Decline of Rome.* New Haven: Yale University Press, 1988.

- Maddison, Angus. *The World Economy: A Millennial Perspective.* Paris: Development Centre Of the Organization for Co-operation and Development, 2001.

- McDevitt, April. "Ancient Egypt: the Mythology." March 2008. 08 Aug 2009. http://www.egyptianmyths.net/hathor.htm>.

- Milani-Santarpia, Giovanni. "Julius Caesar." 17 Aug 2009 http://www.mariamilani.com/ancient_rome/Julius_Caesar_Rome.htm

- "Military," *The Oxford Essential Dictionary of the U.S. Military*. New York: Berkley Books, 2001.

- Munroe, Myles. Rediscovering The Kingdom. Shippensburg: Destiny Image Publishers, Inc., 2004.

- Munroe, Myles. *The Most Important Person On Earth: The Holy Spirit, Governor of the Kingdom*. New Kensington: The Whitaker House, 2007.

- Murdock, Mike. *Seeds of Wisdom on the Holy Spirit*. Volume 14. Denton: The Wisdom Center, 2001.

- Murray, Andrew. *A Life of Power*. New Kensington: Whitaker House, 2002.

- Musser, Donald, and Joseph L. Price, eds. *A New Handbook of Christian Theology*. Nashville: Abingdon Press, 1992.

- Nankin, Jesse. *History of U.S. Government Bailouts*. Pro-Publica, April 15, 2009. http://bailout.propublica.org/.

- "Nelson Mandela." *Wikipedia, The Free Encyclopedia*. 5 Jul 2009, 21:36 UTC. 5 Jul 2009 <http://en.wikipedia.org/w/index.php?title=Nelson_Mandela&oldid=300478382>.

- Ogilivie, Lloyd John. *The Magnificent Vision: Seeing Yourself through the Eyes of Christ*. Ann Arbor: Servant Publications, 1980.

BIBLIOGRAPHY

- Omer-Cooper, J. D. *History of Southern Africa*. Claremont: David Philip Publisher (Pty) Ltd, 1987.

- Osborne, David. *Reinventing Government*. Reading, MA: Addison-Wesley Publishing Company, 1992.

- Patterson, R.D. and Hermann Austel. *Expositor's Bible Commentary, Frank E. Gabelein Ed.* Grand Rapids, MI: Zondervan Publishing House, 1988.

- Pfanner, Eric. Iceland Is All But Officially Bankrupt. *The New York Times*. 19 Oct. 2008.

- Rich, Tracey. "What is Judaism?" <u>Judaism 101 Website</u>. 1995. 08 Aug 2009 <http://www.jewfaq.org/judaism.htm>

- Riley, Pat. *The Royal Priesthood*. Lithonia, GA: New Revelation Publishers, 2006.

- Robertson, Pat. *The Secret Kingdom*. Nashville: Thomas Nelson Publishing, 1982.

- Sack, Kevin. "The Short End of a Longer Life." *The New York Times Online*. 27 April 2009. 08 Aug 2009. <http://www.nytimes.com/2008/04/27/weekinreview/27sack.html?_r=1>.

- Scripture references marked Amplified are taken from the HOLY BIBLE, AMPLIFIED VERSION®. Copyright © 1984 by the International Bible Society. Used by permission of Zondervan Publishing House. All rights reserved.

- Scripture references marked KJV are taken from the HOLY

BIBLE, KING JAMES VERSION®. Copyright © 1977 by the Southwestern Company. Used by permission of Zondervan Bible Publishers. All rights reserved.

• Scripture references marked New Living Translation and Worldwide English (New Testament) are taken from the Biblegate.com Website®. New York. Copyright © 1995-2009 by Zondervan Corporation, LLC. Used by permission of Zondervan Bible Publishers. All rights reserved.

• Smith, Jonathan Z., Ed. *The HarperCollins Dictionary of Religion*. San Francisco: HarperSanFrancisco, 1995.

• Smith, Michael. "What Happened to Our Abundance?" Finance Seminar: World Changer's Church International. College Park, GA. Feb 2009. ZNP, LLC.

• Schofield, Lyle. "Missing the Meaning of Healthcare Reform." Ischofield Web Site. July 2009. 08 Aug 2009. <http://www.ischofield.net/2009/07/missing-the-meaning-of-healthcare-reform/.htm>.

• Strong, James. *The New Strong's Expanded Exhaustive Concordance of the Bible*. Nashville: Thomas Nelson Publishers, 2001.

• Tenney, Merrill C. *New Testament Survey*. Grand Rapids: Wm. B. Eerdmans Publishing Company Inter-Varsity Press, 1985.

• *The Kairos Document: Challenge To The Church*. Braamfontein: The Kairos Theologians, 1986.

BIBLIOGRAPHY

- *The New York Times.* "Adding Up the Government Bailout". 4 Feb. 2009.

- "The U. S. Health Care System." Bureau of Labor Education, University of Maine. Orono, ME. 2001.

- Thomas, Cathy Booth. "Behind The Enron Scandal". *Time Magazine.* Dallas, 2002 June 18.

- Tristam, Pierre. "Jihad: Middle East Issues." 2009. http://middleeast.about.com/od/religionsectarianism/g/me080122a.htm

- Trudeau, Kevin. *Natural Cures "They" Don't Want You To Know About.* Elk Grove Village: Alliance Publishing Group, Inc., 2007.

- United States Department of Labor. (2007 February 27). Health Care Industry Information. Retrieved June 17, 2007 from http://www.doleta.gov/BRG/Indprof/Health.cfm

- Ware, Timothy. *The Orthodox Church.* New York: Penguin Books, 1963.

- Wilbur, Ken. *The Spectrum of Consciousness.* Wheaton, Il: Theosophical Publishing House, 1977.

- World Health Organization. 2009. 08 Aug 2009. <http://www.who.int/about/copyright/en/>.

CPSIA information can be obtained at www.ICGtesting.com
Printed in the USA
LVOW080507261012

304414LV00001B/218/P

9 780986 015991